"Avremi's book is a gift to survivors everywhere and an open and vulnerable firsthand look into what so many experience inside America's judicial system. I felt every emotion reading his story, from heartache for a small boy, to tears of relief when the verdict was announced. I've always had the deepest of respect for Avremi but now my respect and admiration know no bounds."

Elizabeth Smart
New York Times bestselling author of *My Story*
Globally acclaimed advocate

"Beautifully written. Thoughtful and courageous. Avremi tells his story in a compelling, sometimes painful, but ultimately extraordinarily hopeful and positive way."

Chris Stewart
Multiple *New York Times* bestselling author

"My wish, as a veteran sex crimes and child abuse prosecutor, is that every police officer and prosecutor who handles crimes against children would read this book. The Rabbi's words offer powerful lessons for those of us who hold the most sacred of trusts: the safety of children. He offers valuable insight into how victims process sexual abuse, starting with recognition that they were victimized, and how survivors perceive the criminal justice system. Avremi beautifully conveys the power and significance to simply feeling heard and believed by criminal justice professionals. Avremi's perspectives on his relationship with the prosecutor and the detective throughout the case could be a how-to manual for police and prosecutors. In my interactions with survivors of these crimes, I will strive to keep in mind Avremi's perspectives. After all, we in the system can never guarantee a verdict, but we can promise survivors of sex crimes that we will treat each one with respect and dignity, which is a resounding theme of this book. It is my hope that those who read this book will take to heart the gentle guidance offered—and that they will share it with others in our profession."

Assistant United States Attorney Kristina M. Korobov
Southern District of Indiana

"Avremi powerfully recounts his survival of childhood abuse and his courageous decades-long struggle to reconcile with his trauma and the undeserved feelings of shame and inadequacy as he boldly stands up to the perpetrator who preyed on his youthful innocence. His inspiring perspective will benefit other survivors of abuse and the loved ones who search for the words and actions to give them support. His willing bravery to face public scrutiny and ridicule to stand up to his abuser is an act of service and sacrifice to countless victims of abuse who suffer alone. May his courage make their path less lonely and more sure."

Ben McAdams
Former United States Congressman

"Avremi's story is one of great vulnerability and strength. His bravery in telling a story unlike others in the space and the authenticity to share his innermost thoughts have the potential to inspire people for years to come."

Kara Robinson Chamberlain
Survivor and advocate

Not What I Expected

A 20-YEAR JOURNEY TO RECLAIM A CHILD'S VOICE

AVREMI ZIPPEL

Fedd Books
P.O. Box 341973
Austin, TX 78734
www.thefeddagency.com

Published in association with The Fedd Agency, Inc., a literary agency.

ISBN: 978-1-957616-21-6
eIBSN: 978-1-957616-22-3

LCCN: 2023900303

Cover design by Mackenna Cotten
Photography by Melissa Majchrzak

Printed in the United States of America

To Immanuel, Menachem, Sholom
and their future siblings—
I hope this makes you proud.

To my brother and sister survivors—
this one's for you.

1

They're In

November 15, 2019
11:45 a.m.

My face basks in the glow of the cool sunlight of a beautiful Salt Lake City morning.

I've barely been outside all week, so while the rest of my team waits inside, I venture out front and, for the first time in a very long time, attempt to experience life like a normal person.

We know we have a long wait ahead of us; we just don't know how long. "Ninety minutes is the absolute minimum," Donna explained, always providing answers to our questions before we asked them. "Trust me, they get lunch on the state's dime they don't want to pass that up. Just ordering it and eating takes an hour at least. But I've seen this process take several hours."

Shabbat, the Jewish day of rest, starts at sundown. For us, that means that if this takes all day and it gets dark by the time we are dismissed, we will be walking home. As always, my mother comes prepared. She has a change of clothes for us, walking shoes, and a plan—Annie will drive ahead of us, tell everyone the news, and then follow us home. But after the longest, most draining week of my life, every bone in my body hopes it won't come to that.

I pull out my phone to check the time and shake my head—

7

12:05 p.m. Time is creeping forward, each minute lasting a lifetime. I sit in front of the District Attorney's office, responding to all the people who have sent me encouragement throughout the week, laughing at stupid social media posts, and carelessly people watching.

Eventually, I get up and head inside to rejoin the rest of the team.

The lobby of the D.A.'s office is not the most welcoming place—bulletproof windows, cold hard benches, and bright fluorescent lights. And yet, by this point, it almost feels homey. Or, at the very least, familiar.

At one o'clock, Donna walks into the conference room with an ever-present smile. "How's everyone doing?"

"They haven't asked about the phone call yet," I say quickly, hoping for a crumb of optimism that things are trending in the right direction. "That's good news, right?"

"Well, actually," Donna says, as my face falls, "they did call us back in about the phone call. I just got out about fifteen minutes ago."

My stomach, hopefully residing somewhere between its usual resting place and my upper chest, crashes through the rest of my body and hurtles through the floor.

They wanted to hear the phone call again?

They actually bought that garbage that she couldn't hear?

Is this really happening?

Donna must have noticed the look on my face. "I wouldn't worry about it, Avremi. It could actually be . . ."

I'm sure the rest of what Donna has to say is great, but we never hear it. Her phone, placed very conspicuously on the table, begins vibrating rather prominently. It's an 801 number. One she doesn't have saved in her contacts.

As her phone shakes, the rest of the room goes still. I hold my breath as she picks up.

"Donna? It's Becky. They're in."

Those final two words hang in the air for a quick moment, followed by a jolt of energy that shocks us all as we leap to our feet. Those two words are going to close the book.

"They're in" will be the culmination of 90 minutes.

"They're in" will be the culmination of 4 days.

"They're in" will be the culmination of 22 months.

"They're in" will be the culmination of over 20 years.

This is it. After everything I've been through—they are in.

2

A Controlled Environment

Spring 1998

Life is about something greater than yourself. I learned this at a very young age.

As observant Jews, my family centered everything in our home and in our lives around Torah values. You have a mission, a purpose, and a sense of responsibility toward something larger.

It also meant strict do's and don'ts.

Every single thing we put in our mouths was Kosher.

Daily prayer wasn't just recommended; it was required.

And Shabbat started as soon as the sun set every Friday evening, which meant no phones, no devices, no cooking, no driving—nothing that resembled work—for twenty-five hours.

I grew up with the sense that there was *our* world, and then there was *their* world—the outside world. A place generally categorized as "immodest" and "inappropriate." Full of countless outside influences that had no place in our house.

Monitoring what we let in became very important.

I've always loved sports, especially basketball. But live broadcasts meant unfiltered commercials, and that was a dangerous game, so I grew up watching the Utah Jazz a day behind. We had a family friend who recorded the games and brought them over so I could watch them while skipping commercials.

Like I said, a controlled environment.

It might seem foreign to you. Likely it does. For me, it was all I knew at that phase of my life, and I wholeheartedly embraced it. I had no resentments toward it then, nor do I now. I consider myself blessed to be in a position where I can choose to raise my own children with the same values.

My family was an independent ecosystem. We were a cruise ship floating through sea. While the rest of the world was busy doing their thing, we were doing ours.

Instead of going to school, we were homeschooled. As my siblings and I joke, we were doing the cool thing before the rest of the kids started. I guess we've always just been ahead of our time.

Our mom was our teacher. She also ran our household with the precision of an entire Secret Service advance team. Instead of a dozen agents, it was all her.

Very few things happened she didn't know about.

My father has been the Rabbi of our community for my entire life. While my mom was running our home, he was always out running around—meeting with people, encouraging people, praying with people. From a young age, I always found that idea appealing. That felt like the most important thing you could dedicate your life to.

The responsibility.

The sense of power.

The opportunity to speak to the community, communicate, and educate.

To be seen as a person who had something to give and to be someone whose input was welcomed and appreciated at every juncture.

For as long as I can remember, I wanted to be a Rabbi like him.

Growing up, I spent a lot of my afternoons volunteering in the synagogue.

This was before emails were a thing, so we used to mail our regular newsletters to everyone in the community. In those days, that was a lot more complicated than hitting send on a computer. We'd print them out, put them in envelopes, and stick a label with a different mailing address to each one. The USPS also mandated we separate each envelope by zip code, so we'd spend hours stacking letters in different piles, putting a sticker on each stack to indicate where to take it.

While other kids were at school learning in a classroom and navigating how to interact with their peers on the playground, I was learning about the US Postal Service.

———

Just after I turned seven years old, my fourth sibling was born. Our little family now had the makings of a basketball team with a deep bench. As controlled as our home was, it was chaotic—five kids, each with a seemingly endless amount of energy.

We needed help. Someone to take care of all the kids while my mom focused on our education.

At first we cycled through a few different part-time caregivers, but they didn't stick around long. With such a unique home, we were asking a lot from any nanny. Chances were they'd have to pivot from their preferences and values and learn a whole new way of life that we call observant Judaism.

It took some time, but we finally found someone who seemed up for the challenge.

Her name was Alavina Florreich.

3

A Natural-Born Caregiver

July 1998

Hiring a babysitter was an event in the house.

Since venturing into the "outside" was not super common, adding a new person into our world was a big deal.

Alavina (or as we started calling her, Vina) did not disappoint.

I'll never forget the first moment she walked up our steps wearing a brown floral shirt, one of several island-based outfits she sported. Her personality matched her attire. She was kind, funny, quick to laugh, and super easygoing—a natural-born caregiver.

We were sold.

Vina quickly became a part of our family. She was in our home every weekday, making us lunch, changing diapers, and putting the younger kids down for naps while my mother taught the older kids.

She learned our ways quickly.

I'm the oldest of six and have always wanted to be older. I saw myself as an adult at the ripe old age of seven and always wanted to be helpful rather than hurtful. In my mind, the best way to do that was to be a conduit of sorts between the adults and the rest of the kids, more of a surrogate parent than a son.

When Vina showed up, I took it upon myself to help her acclimate. Step one was to teach her everything she needed to know about our lifestyle.

Kosher.

Shabbat.

Modesty.

To her credit, Vina picked it up quickly.

She learned all the Jewish standards and doubled down on our values, taking great pride in being a part of the ecosystem. She knew we didn't do mixed swimming, so instead of taking us to the neighborhood pool after our studies, she'd take us to the park. Whenever she'd bring us to the store to buy a snack, she'd remind us of the rules of Kosher (even though we were well aware of them).

Vina didn't just put up with our culture, she embraced and enhanced it. She played by the rules and helped us feel an even deeper sense of pride in our lifestyle.

And that's exactly how she started taking advantage of me.

4

Don't Tell Anybody

September 1999

My eighth birthday party is my first memory in our new home.

When our family outgrew our first house, we moved a few blocks down the street to a slightly bigger home. Up until that point, I never had any privacy. When you live in a small house with lots of siblings, it comes with the territory—I was never alone. In our new place, that changed. It was bigger and had a finished basement with multiple rooms separated by a long hallway.

For the first time in my life, privacy was possible.

As an observant young man reaches eight or nine, it's an important time. The lines you draw between the genders get taken up a notch. After eight, boys and girls stop exchanging intentional, physical contact with members of the other gender outside their immediate family.

No hugging.

No touching.

Nothing.

At all.

Full stop.

However, Vina was a deeply affectionate person. Hugs and pats on the back were normal for her, and she gave them to us so frequently that I never felt weird or strange about it. She quickly became the one exception in my life.

One day, Vina and I were alone in the basement, and she encouraged me to give her a massage.

A massage?

I had a vague idea what that was, but the request was so discombobulating that I didn't know what to say. In silent motion, I stood up and walked behind the couch and started rubbing her shoulders, following her instructions as I went.

It was a strange feeling.

But it was also exhilarating.

My hands were moving, my heart was racing, and my ears were straining, listening for any movement that may signal my mom or a sibling coming down the stairs.

Is this okay?

Is this allowed?

Slowly but surely, the massages became commonplace. Anytime we were alone, watching or reading something downstairs, we would rub each other's shoulders. It was the first gray area I ever really experienced in my life.

Did my parents forbid the massages? No.

Did they know about the massages? Also no.

What would they say if they found out? I wasn't sure.

For the next few months, I didn't say a word to anyone, signaling to Vina that I would keep my mouth shut. Looking back, it feels like the massages were a test case of sorts for her, and I passed with flying colors.

The word "grooming" gets thrown around a lot today, and as is typically the case, when a word is spread thin, it becomes ambiguous. But it's the right word for what happened.

Vina played the long game; she moved slowly. You have to do that with an eight-year-old Orthodox boy who gets nervous watching Disney movies if it seems like a kissing scene is on the horizon. You don't jump straight across the line; you slowly nudge it—one foot massage, one shoulder rub, one comment at a time.

Until one afternoon in September of 1999.

We were downstairs watching a movie again. Vina was lying on her side on our couch, and I was positioned behind her, rubbing her shoulders, an act that was normalized in my mind at this point. Suddenly she reached up, took my hand, brought it beneath her shirt line, and placed it on her (covered) breast.

I froze.

Life stopped before me.

She held my hand there, lingering for a moment, and when I pulled back to move it away, she didn't resist.

Instinctively, I knew what I did was wrong. Very wrong. But I didn't run. I didn't panic. I didn't yell. In fact, I didn't say anything. I had no idea what the appropriate response should be, so I just internalized the event and went right back to rubbing her shoulders.

Over the next few days, I lived in a state of shock.

The good person in my life made me cross a boundary. What do I do with that?

My entire household was designed to keep me from doing something like this. We didn't watch the commercials during Jazz games so we wouldn't be exposed to this sort of thing. We stayed away from public pools so we wouldn't be tempted by this sort of stuff.

The bad stuff.

Not just inappropriate.

Not a gray area.

Bad.

I grew up with a strict sense that there are good things you do and bad things you don't do, no questions asked. I had one job to do—stay away from the bad ones—and I failed miserably.

What should I do now? Should I tell someone?

I certainly wasn't going to tell my dad. He was a Rabbi—he was the man I aspired to be. Or, I should say, he was the man I aspired to be until I threw it all away that afternoon.

I knew I couldn't tell my mom. She'd turn our house upside down if she knew what happened in the basement of her own home. If I thought I had strict boundaries at that point, I couldn't imagine what would happen if she found out.

Siblings? No way. All five of them looked up to me. They needed me to be their older brother. I knew they could never know.

———

Vina never told me not to tell. She never needed to.

There's something so misunderstood about imbalanced power dynamics. Because the sway is so strong, much of the communication is nonverbal.

You want a kid to really keep a secret for you? Don't even bother mentioning that they shouldn't tell. The very fact that an adult has brought them into their inner sanctum should be enough to guarantee their silence.

At no point in any of our lifetimes did Vina ever look me in the eye and say "don't tell anyone." Not at the beginning, middle, or end. She didn't need to.

Normalizing physical touch between the two of us in the most innocuous of circumstances was the wedge. That was the test case. Looking back, you have to marvel at the brilliance. If I say something, the encounters are innocent enough to just explain away. And if I don't? Then we're in business.

I remember the first time she asked me for a foot rub. I hesitated.

Clearly, I knew it was wrong. That's where she applied the pressure. "C'mon, it's okay. It's just a little rub!" I can only imagine the wheels turning in her head as she watched my defense mechanisms fall.

Suddenly, I held something dangerous in my hands. A secret. It felt so adultlike to know a secret. This wasn't a surprise birthday party, however, or that my mommy had a baby in her belly. Even my parents didn't know about this questionable thing I had done.

What do I do with it?

Do I tell?

I knew I probably shouldn't, that it would only get me in trouble. And even if I did decide to tell, it didn't have to be today or tomorrow.

I'll get around to it at some point.

For now, I just wanted to enjoy feeling so big and mature.

So what did I do? I kept my mouth shut. Out of a misguided sense of self-preservation.

As long as I kept up the appearance of the "perfect child," I was one less headache to be dealt with—a far more appealing possibility from my vantage point.

But to keep up appearances, I would have to keep my mouth shut.

There was only one adult in my life who could ever know about this— and so I ran right back to her.

Over and over again.

5

A Place and
A Pattern

1999-2004

To this day, the roses are imprinted on my mind—the outdated floral design on the nasty wallpaper in our dark, dingy downstairs bathroom.

It was claustrophobic, even for a child. Besides a toilet and a sink, there was no other furniture. There was barely any room to move, and the walls always felt like they were closing in around you.

My mom ran every square inch of our house. As such, she made it clear there were certain areas you were allowed in and other areas you had no business in. The basement bathroom was definitely the latter. It was right next to the downstairs guest room and was reserved for our guests when they stayed with us. Vina was the only other person who was allowed to use it. All of us kids were to stay out.

I never once remember actually using the bathroom.

But I did spend a lot of time in it.

When I was in that tiny space, I was out of my mom's sight. I was separated from my siblings by a wall and a long hallway that would begin to feel like a plank I couldn't stop walking down. A plank that signaled I was jumping off the boat of my childhood innocence and submerging into a dark sea of isolation and shame.

That bathroom is the loneliest place I've ever been, even though I was never in there alone. Vina was always with me.

As soon as each episode began, I would stare at the roses on the wall in an attempt to check out of my own body until it was over.

———

The second episode was where the real problem began.

Began being the operative word.

The initial episode came out of nowhere; there wasn't much I could've done to prevent it. I didn't know how to respond. I didn't have the tools to understand what happened, the support system to process, or the language to even know where to begin.

From my own experiences and having worked with hundreds of survivors, I've learned over the years that if the first episode goes unaddressed, it's almost a guarantee that there will be a second episode.

That's certainly what happened to me.

Everyone loved Vina. She was larger than life and appeared to care about our family so much. She'd sit with us during family meals, and we'd all laugh together like one big, happy family.

Then the two of us would sneak down to the basement bathroom.

No eight-year-old is prepared to process the pain or confusion attached to a sexual experience, let alone an eight-year-old who fast-forwards through the kissing scene in *The Little Mermaid*.

I was so confused.

I had no idea what was happening.

And the shame I felt was palpable and miserable—it engulfed me.

I must be the world's biggest screwup.

———

That's when the survival techniques began.

I became so cautious and careful to make sure that no one suspected anything was wrong that I would withdraw into myself. I stayed away from people, specifically Vina, never looking her in the eyes for more than a quick glance before shifting my eyes back down to the floor.

When I was around, I was extra helpful, extra kind, and extra sweet, just to keep up the appearance that everything was on the up and up. This was especially true around my parents, as they were the ones who most needed to be assured that nothing was potentially wrong.

I only knew two things for certain. The first was that I didn't want another episode to happen again, and the second was that I knew it would.

For the first time in my life, something was happening to me that I couldn't stop.

Life snatched control away from me.

My new life mission became finding a way to get that control back.

6

Shame

Spring 2004

אשמנו, בגדנו, גזלנו, דברנו דפי.

Per usual, I left the bathroom before Vina. As I walked back up the dimly lit basement hallway to rejoin my siblings in the playroom, I muttered the confessional prayer in Hebrew, knowing full well how many laws I had just broken.

This must be the fiftieth time I've prayed this prayer. How many more before God's patience runs out?

That small, cramped, windowless hell had become my torture chamber. And the walk back down the hallway had become the walk of shame. The shame I felt was miserable, palpable. Nearly impossible to put into words.

It hit in waves.

Intense grief and sadness were first—the feeling you get when you finish a sad movie, but intensified by the understanding that instead of this being a fictional story, it was real life, and you brought it on yourself. A cloud of doom would set in around me. Each step felt like trudging through a dense raincloud.

Did I really just do that again? I'm such a failure, such a waste of a life. God must hate me.

The sadness didn't last forever; eventually, it would be overrun by grief and profound self-loathing.

I'm such an idiot. I swore I'd never be back. How could I be so dull?

Then I'd see my siblings playing so innocently, and the purity of my surroundings shamed me. My parents set up my entire life to protect me from these mistakes. I imagined how disappointed they'd be if they found out.

The next phase of the shame was the line I'd draw in the sand. At some point, I'd take my stand and promise God that I would never, ever, under any circumstance, be back.

Just give me one more chance—a fresh start. I promise I won't ruin this one.

But of course, those types of stands hold more power the first few times you make them. Each episode made that promise feel less and less sincere, forcing me to double down with tears and make the next promise that much more grandiose. In reality, this just meant the next time I returned to the downstairs bathroom, I'd punish myself and lash out at myself even worse.

Over the years, the self-pity grew and the self-hatred became harsher and harsher—all in an attempt to overcompensate for the last broken promise.

And the one before that.

And the one before that.

However, no matter how extreme or intense the inner turmoil got, it paled in comparison to the danger of what faced me in the rest of the house. The fear of being found out was worse than any inner battle I faced.

After every episode, my anxious mind would start racing.

Did anyone see us? Does anyone know? I would've heard them coming down the stairs, right? They would've said something by now. Surely we're in the clear.

———

From a young age, I mastered how to compartmentalize everything I felt. I had to learn to build drawers in my mind where I could stuff the memory of the actual events. And then another drawer where I could keep the sadness. A third where I could keep the shame. A fourth for all the fear.

Because a few minutes after each episode, I was surrounded by my big, happy, innocent, Chabad family. I was thrust right back into Kosher meals and Torah study. No matter how intense all those emotions got, I had to train myself to stuff them down. And if they no longer fit in the mental compartment I had for each one, I built a bigger one.

There was a progression to the intensity and seriousness of the acts Vina and I were participating in, but simultaneously, there was a progression to the complexity of the compartments I was shoving all this into.

My denial grew alongside the abuse.

For years, I'd throw those feelings into their place, close the drawer, and turn the lock. Then I'd head back to the dinner table and continue the charade that nothing was wrong.

Somewhere in the deep, dark recesses of my mind, the truth was raging, screaming, pleading to have its day, to see some light. But it was buried by so many levels of lies that no one could hear its pleas.

Not even me.

I could hate myself from today until tomorrow—that was all fine and good. But no one could ever find out about this.

———

Eventually, after cycling through just about every negative emotion you can think of, my mind and body would go numb—I'd become almost robotic. I was unable to process what just happened, what I knew was going to happen, and what I still could not stop.

I welcomed the numbness.

Feeling nothing became the preferred emotion over all the other options.

And then it would happen all over again.

There's a good chance a lot of this doesn't make sense to you. If that's you, consider yourself lucky.

There's a reason why abusing a child is so heinous. You take them out of the realm of normal for the rest of their lives. What's normal and sensible and rational to you in this moment was unattainable for me at that point. The ability to process the situation and dilemma had been taken from me by the trauma, and there seemed like no way to get it back.

I was young, isolated, and alone.

7

The Airport Loop

2004-2012

I spent my teenage years stuck in a loop.

Whenever I was home for the summer, episodes were inevitable. Sometimes Vina and I went a few weeks or even a month between them. But if she was at our house and I was close by, it was only a matter of time before we made our way back to the downstairs bathroom.

Fortunately, every fall brought a much-needed reprieve.

The path to becoming a Rabbi is long and challenging, which was exactly what I needed to distract myself from those compartments of shame buried deep in my soul. The journey brought me to lots of different schools around the country and the world. Every September, I'd pack my bags, hug my family, and risk a quick glance at Vina before averting my eyes. Then I'd head to the Salt Lake City International Airport and head off to outthink and outrun my pain.

At the airport, my trauma slowly moved away from the present and settled into my past, and I welcomed the shift. Being a teenager is hard enough. Being a teenager in a very religious household where you are secretly being sexually abused by the nanny everyone else loves and trusts is a particularly cruel form of torment.

As I waited to board the plane, I took great care to stuff the bad, sick, evil, deranged version of myself deep in a pit to make sure that the perfect version of myself who was training to be a Rabbi could shine in all of its glory.

When I arrived at Yeshiva, I threw myself into my studies. My self-worth was at an all-time low, and academics were the one place I had left where I could shine. I finally had something back in my life I could control, and I grasped onto it as tightly as I could with everything I had.

Academic perfection became my new vice; I couldn't afford to be a normal, average, run-of-the-mill student. A 98 on a test wasn't going to cut it. The second-best grade in the class wasn't enough. Deep down, I feared that if I wasn't seen as the best or the brightest, I'd be found out for who I really was.

A fraud.

A fake.

Immoral.

Unclean.

Unfit to be a Rabbi.

There's a reason so many trauma survivors struggle with forms of OCD. It's our desire to exercise control, to find a sliver of life where we aren't susceptible to the power that someone or something else has over us.

Slipping grades is one of the possible symptoms of child abuse.

But I discovered the opposite could also be true. Drowning yourself in your studies can be just as toxic as running away from them.

Both are cries for help from a broken soul.

———

Yeshiva was my reprieve from the episodes, but that didn't mean it was a reprieve from the shame. Rabbinical school places a strong emphasis on taking time for introspection and being aware of where you truly are in life.

Those times were torturous for me.

Any moment given to self-refinement, betterment of one's ways, or being a better, more spiritual, more aligned version of myself was fertile breeding ground for the worst thoughts in the world to dance on center stage.

"It's imperative we aim to be better versions of ourselves," a Rabbi in Yeshiva said. My classmates nodded in unison, and I did too. Meanwhile, my inner voices of self-loathing mocked me.

Do you think you're like them? You're not. You're the only one struggling with this. Do you really think you stand a chance of making any effort to improve your life? Do you realize what you'll be caught up in the moment you get home however-many days from now? You're not in control of your life.

The inner work was miserable, all the more reason to just focus on academics. I was terrified of slowing down because slowing down meant confronting the things going on beneath the surface.

Instead of doing the inner work, I threw myself at the outer work.

If I can just become a Rabbi, that will fix all this.

———

Every June, I finished another year of Rabbinical school and took another step closer to becoming a Rabbi. But while all my classmates were high-fiving and celebrating, I was mourning, the bleak basement bathroom flashing through my mind.

I'd land in SLC, and my past trauma would start pounding on the door, mocking me.

The party's over. Back to reality.

It was never a question of *if*; it was only a question of *when*. Over any visit home, Vina and I inevitably would find ourselves in the downstairs bathroom, and I lived out the supposed vacation vacillating between self-pity, self-hate, and shame. I spent all of my precious time with my family counting the days until I could get to the airport and put as many miles as possible between Vina and me.

————

When leaving home, I'd get to the airport feeling ashamed about my past. When returning home, I'd get to the airport feeling fearful about my future.

I was caught in a loop.

A vicious cycle.

One that lasted my entire adolescence.

Because the only way out of the loop would've been to let someone else in on what was happening. Speaking up was the prerequisite for regaining control of my life, but it would also mean public humiliation at a level I couldn't comprehend.

If such a thought was ever brave enough to surface, it was quickly stomped down into silence.

I gave up any hope of breaking the cycle.

The loop was too strong.

I was destined to stay caught in it for the rest of my life.

————

By the summer of 2009, our family grew out of our need for Vina. All my siblings were old enough to fend for themselves at that point, so it was time to say goodbye.

That was a difficult goodbye for the rest of them. There were lots of tearful hugs, kisses, and promises to stay in touch.

My mind was elsewhere. As I said goodbye, I was determined to make sure that this never happened again and that no one would ever find out about it. I wished Vina well and watched her leave, promising myself that I would take all those moments we shared in the downstairs bathroom to the grave.

8

The Stairwell

November 15, 2019
1:05 p.m.

My mind races.

They're in.

This entire journey has led me here. Nothing more can be done. Nothing more can be said. For better or worse, the jury has made its decision.

We have ten minutes to get back to the courtroom, and Donna's office looks like the sideline during the fourth quarter of the Super Bowl. Everyone paces around nervously, exchanging concerned looks and talking louder than they probably need to.

"Get back here now. They're in!" my mother says into her phone.

Twenty minutes earlier, my father had given into real life and headed back to the office to prepare for Shabbat.

"He just parked his car back at the synagogue," she says, flustered. Then she glances back at me with a reassuring smile. "Don't worry. He'll make it back."

Don't worry? He'll just have to break every speeding law and potentially run a few lights to get back in time. But sure, I won't worry.

Word spreads quickly among my siblings; before we even have a chance to leave Donna's office, our family's group text blows up with

GIFs, emojis, and pleas to my mom to leave her phone on during the verdict so they can hear it live.

"We will not be committing any felonies in a courtroom!" my mother yells into her phone through gritted teeth.

They are out of luck, and they know it. As they have done all week long, they will have to suffice with a text update to find out how it's all going down.

I need to break away from the pack and get away from it all.

The noise.

The chaos.

My team is amazing. I'm so thankful for all of them and the ways they have had my back during this journey, but I need to do this final leg on my own.

I leave Donna's office and make the walk to the Matheson Courthouse one last time. This time by myself.

Most people will be using the front entrance to the building again, but I don't care about that anymore. I have no strength left for nostalgia, no energy to be sentimental. My final task is to make it up to the fourth floor, back to Judge Trease's courtroom, where I will hear the verdict at long last.

Keys, phone, belt, wallet.

I try to count how many times I've gone through security this week. Let alone this month. Or in my twenty-eight years on Earth. My hands have gotten so used to taking off my belt and emptying my pockets that I can do it in one fluid motion.

Why is this so normal for me?

Why do I feel so comfortable in a building that is so strange to so many?

I'm not a lawyer. I may have thought about becoming one, but I'm not.

None of this should've happened. But it did, and here we are, finally making it to the finish line.

There is an elevator up to the fourth floor, but it seems fitting to take the stairs one last time. For all the love, support, help, and advocacy I've had along the way, this journey ends the way it started.

With me.

Alone.

The same way I sat in that downstairs bathroom for what seemed like hours.

Crying.

Praying.

Trying to find the courage to get back up and face the day.

I crack open the door and enter, embracing the all-too-familiar feeling. Cold. Dark. Uninviting. And yet, quiet.

The only thing in front of me is a seemingly endless flight of stairs.

So I begin the climb, the same way it has gone for twenty years. Just me and eight-year-old Avremi, finding our footing in this dance of life.

One step.

Then another.

And then another.

Perhaps if I climb long enough, I'll get to where I am going. Perhaps if I put in enough work, enough effort, I'll reach the thing I am longing for. Maybe I'll be able to climb out of the darkness I thought I'd be surrounded by forever and finally find some light.

Instead, each step seems to leave me feeling more isolated.

All I want is to go to bat for my younger self, but I had no idea it would be a nearly impossible journey. It feels like some cruel joke. The effort wasn't fixing my problems, just reminding me how deep I had fallen—and how alone I truly was.

But the effort was also the only way forward, the only solution I could think of. So for years, I just kept climbing.

Step after step.

Floor after floor.

9

"You Must be Sheina"

October 1, 2013

I took a deep, slow inhale and an even longer exhale, trying everything I could to calm my nerves as I glanced down at the clock in my rented Nissan Altima.

6:58 p.m.

Two minutes early.

So far, so good.

Dating looks a little different in my community. Remember, from age eight or nine, we don't have any contact with members of the opposite gender. At least we're not supposed to. This means dating is less about going out and meeting someone and more about your family introducing you to someone.

I'm often asked if my community believes in "arranged marriages," and if, in fact, my wife and I had been "arranged." The way I see it, it's far more analogous to a blind date.

Someone you trust thinks you'll enjoy the company of someone else, and once the two of you meet, you enter an environment where both of you dictate terms every step of the way moving forward. There's no part that exists without the express consent of you and your new friend.

In our case, during my last year of Rabbinical school, one of my favorite teachers began to notice that I might be a good fit for his younger sister, Sheina. After he told his mom about me, she approached my mom. My parents agreed to "look into the idea" (the natural progression in our circles). Apparently both families approved, because I was told to be outside an apartment building in Brooklyn, New York, on Tuesday at 7 p.m.

Like I said, dating looks a little different for us.

I've always had a way with words, but when the passenger door swung open and Sheina hopped in, my typically quick mind failed me. I uttered four words she's never let me live down.

"You must be Sheina."

Smooth.

To be fair, I was twenty-two, had never been on a date, and hadn't really held a conversation with a girl in fourteen years. But neither my family nor hers lets me forget it.

Fortunately, things got better after my opening line. We hung out for about four hours that night and thoroughly enjoyed each other's company. When we got back to Crown Heights, the Brooklyn neighborhood we both called home at the time, we each reported back to our parents and decided to go out again on Thursday.

Date number two lasted even longer.

I liked her. A lot. She was attractive, funny, sweet, and a great listener. We quickly realized we had a tremendous amount in common and never seemed to run out of things to talk about.

We went out again on Sunday—the third time in five days. After an amazing five-hour date, which included a long walk along the East River in Manhattan, I told my mother that Sheina was the girl I wanted to marry.

Date number four was the following Wednesday. As we walked past Times Square and stood in front of *Ripley's Believe It or Not*, I knew the time was right.

I asked her to marry me.

"I'm not sure," she famously responded. "I need some time to think about it."

We had only known each other for eight days, so I figured that was fair. Fortunately, she thought about it pretty quickly, because by the time we drove back to Brooklyn, her answer changed from a *maybe* to a *yes*.

The engagement wasn't just a win for Sheina and me; it was a win for all of our friends and family. In our community, weddings are a source of great joy—a time of immense celebration.

Her family was excited.

Mine was ecstatic.

Our love story was unfolding before our eyes, and for the first time in a long time, I felt a deep sense of hope.

Maybe this is the first step I need to take.

A step to move out of the shame of my past and experience a real, intimate relationship in a healthy way.

And so the wedding was upon us. Perhaps a light flickered at the end of the tunnel.

10

Mazel Tov

January 6, 2014

As Sheina and I stood under the Chuppah on our wedding day, I thought of my mom's father. Even though Zaidy had passed away less than six months ago, I knew my grandfather was still with us.

Jewish weddings begin with a ceremony called a Chuppah. A Chuppah is a wedding canopy the bride and groom stand under, representing the home they are creating together. These ceremonies are always intense, meaningful, and emotional.

But for me, the moment was extra heavy.

The Chuppah ceremony is a time to remember and honor deceased loved ones, so naturally I reflected on my grandfather's life.

My Zaidy was one of the smartest people I ever met. He was an accomplished author and a gifted orator—a communicator of unmatched skill. He was my main motivation for developing my passion in public speaking. Since I had been a boy, I wanted to be just like him.

In the summer of 2010, he was diagnosed with the most aggressive and deadly form of brain cancer. The doctors gave him six to twelve months to live. In typical Zaidy fashion, he battled back and went on to live three full years after his diagnosis.

Zaidy spent the entirety of his Rabbinic career in Toronto, Canada, and he lived out his final days there as well. At the time, I was wrapping up my Rabbinic ordination a short flight away in New Jersey, so I had the privilege of spending a significant amount of my time caring for him.

When I flew out to Toronto for Passover in 2013, I witnessed the cruelest and most ironic twist of fate. As things worsened, he was primarily affected by an inability to communicate his thoughts verbally.

The illness was taking away one of his greatest gifts.

There was no doubt that his mind was working just fine, but the great orator was losing his ability to translate those thoughts into understandable words.

At the First Seder, the feast that begins Passover, I did my best to let Zaidy lead and finish his sentences enough that he could feel that he was giving over his own thoughts. I'll never forget the sad smile he offered me at one such effort. He knew we were all doing our best and appreciated that, but it wasn't the same.

The following day, I tried to push him to the synagogue in a wheelchair so that he could join his community for the holiday services. He was visibly agitated on the ride, and as we got there, he became increasingly deregulated, so much so that we decided to bring him home early.

By the time we got home, we knew something was wrong and called an ambulance to take him to the hospital.

The hours in the emergency room at Mount Sinai Hospital are etched into my memory forever. My grandmother and I sat there silently, looking over to check on him every couple of minutes. At one point, I noticed he was speaking even though no one was around, and when I went over to see what was going on, my stomach rose in my throat.

He was saying the Shema, one of the final prayers recited on a deathbed.

This wasn't the same man who had been beside himself in a wheelchair hours before. He was making his final stand. His voice rang out clear and strong as he chanted the words as if he was reading them straight out of a prayer book.

When I took his hand in mine, he squeezed my fingers with a strength that had failed him since before his diagnosis.

My Zaidy, my hero, was saying goodbye.

He finished praying and looked me square in the eye, his face gleaming with peace. "You should be happy and healthy, and you should keep your mommy happy and healthy, and definitely Bubby [my grandmother]; you'll need to keep her happy and healthy, and you should have lots of beautiful children . . ."

I choked back a sob.

He never did get to finish that thought because my grandmother had observed the action and came charging over. Hearing the exchange, she saw precisely where this was going and interjected.

"No, no, no, stop this right now. I don't want to hear any more of this."

He turned to her and began blowing her kisses, and I withdrew to let them sort that out one last time.

Zaidy lived three more months, but that exchange was my goodbye.

When Sheina and I began to date, I shared this story with her. It was the first death I'd experienced in my adult life, and it left a hole. It introduced me to a new kind of sadness, one I'd get to know rather well in the years to follow.

I knew Zaidy would have loved Sheina. And I knew he'd be at the wedding with us.

Jewish mysticism teaches that the souls of the departed join us from their resting places at the joyous occasions of their descendants. That's why the Chuppah ceremony was extra somber for me. I wore Zaidy's raincoat and knew in some deep way that he was there with us.

———

As heavy as the first half of the wedding was for me, the second half felt incredibly liberating. Our weddings oscillate between some pretty extreme emotional experiences. After the solemn Chuppah ceremony, we let loose. We eat, we toast, and we dance.

Jewish scripture tells of the concept of "expungement." "Forgiven for all of your sins," to put it into the textual words. We're taught there are a few rare moments in life when your record gets completely wiped clean. One of these moments comes at a wedding, when a bride and groom are recipients of this rare Divine gift.

As I walked onto the dance floor, I supposed that all brides and grooms need expungement, but I was also convinced that no one needed it more than me. Because beneath my smile and behind my words, I was still convinced God hated me.

I may have given my life to becoming a Rabbi.

I may have committed my life to serving a community.

I may have tried everything I could to climb out of the dark pit of shame I was stuck in.

But deep down, I didn't believe any of that was enough to make up for the years of incidents with Vina. No matter what I did, I felt like I couldn't outrun my sin. No matter how hard I tried, I'd close my eyes and be back in that downstairs bathroom.

Surrounded by fear.

Covered in shame.

And completely alone.

No one knew. Not my parents. Not Sheina. I'd never tell them. I couldn't. I was convinced I'd take my secret to the grave.

Expungement was my only hope for a fresh start. It was my only hope for a new beginning. My wedding wasn't just a chance to begin this new chapter with my wife; it was my chance to leave the old Avremi behind. Sheina's and my souls were going to be united, and all my issues would go up in smoke.

Enough was enough.

I had been spiraling in this deep cycle of shame for too long.

This was supposed to be my moment of freedom and clarity, just like the book says. I danced with such joy that night. This was a golden opportunity, and I wasn't going to squander it. Every negative thing in my life would cease to exist from that night and forever more, and the harder I danced and the more I celebrated, the further away I was sending it.

Surrounded by all my friends, my family, my Zaidy, and my beautiful bride, I danced the night away—hoping beyond hope that I was leaving the old me behind for good.

11

The Magic Potion?

2014

Did it work? Did all my dancing send my past mistakes away? Was God giving me a second chance?

I don't know.

Whether or not the divine expungement was real, I know it didn't make me feel any better. The wedding may have been incredible, but the months that followed were painful.

Since the age of eight, I had lived by the following rules:

No physical contact with anyone of the opposite gender.

No holding hands, even on dates.

No touching, even once you're engaged.

Nothing until the wedding.

That's what we are taught. And all of the above was true for me, with the slight caveat that a woman touched me sexually and made me do the same to her for ten years—and no one knew about it.

After the wedding, however, everything changes. Suddenly intimacy is not just permissible; it's encouraged.

The truth is, even young men and women in my community who

have zero sexual trauma in their background struggle with this in the beginning. It's so beyond the pale our entire lives, and then in a moment, everything changes.

What was forbidden is now celebrated.

What was deemed sinful is now sacred.

And you are expected to flip the switch immediately.

The novelty is a lot for anyone to handle at first.

Compound that with the reality that every time a survivor of sexual violence tries to be intimate, they are brought back to the moment of their abuse, and it made for a brutal cocktail for me.

I hoped beyond hope that marriage would fix everything I was feeling. All I wanted was to experience intimacy in a safe, beautiful, and loving way.

I hoped marriage would be the ultimate palate cleanser, the magic potion that turned a decade of pain and shame into a distant memory. But it turns out, it's not quite that simple.

Marriage wasn't a magic potion.

Instead, it was a revealer. It showed me how poisoned my mind had become.

If my issue was a lack of control, intimacy multiplied it by seventy-five million. It felt like I was dying inside, yet as painful as that was, I made every effort necessary to make sure that pain stayed inside. Sheina could never know.

In Yeshiva, I exercised control by excelling academically. And I wasn't just good; I was great. I was the best. But unfortunately, I wasn't great at marriage. No matter how hard I tried, it wasn't solving my problems. My name wasn't making it to the top of any leaderboard. I thought getting married would be a step out of the shame, but instead, it dragged me further into it.

———

What do you do when the thing you hoped would fix your problems doesn't work? What do you do when you realize your best attempt to climb out of the pit you're in is insufficient?

My answer was to double down and work even harder.

The community I grew up in didn't have space for internal problems. We didn't have time to look inward when there were so many outward hills to climb. Instead, we buried our pain behind our purpose and kept moving forward.

That's exactly what I did.

I excelled at the one thing I could still control—academics. I finished Rabbinical school, and then we decided to move to Utah, where I would fulfill my lifelong dream of becoming a practicing Rabbi.

Surely, once I was a Rabbi, my problems would go away.

Surely serving my community was the solution.

As a Rabbi, I'd be obligated to live a life of outward perfection. And I hoped, more than anything, that all that outward perfection would mask the inward brokenness. I wasn't going to look at the pain; I didn't know how to. The only thing I had mastered was pushing down my pain and taking another step up my proverbial staircase.

So we packed up our apartment, and all three of us got on a plane to Salt Lake City.

I say three because Sheina had just gotten pregnant. We were counting down the days until we got to welcome our first child.

The plane left the airport, and I silently prayed I was leaving behind all my failures of being a husband. As we headed west, I offered Sheina a measly smile and wondered if fatherhood would fix this empty feeling inside me.

12

Fatherhood

July 29, 2015

Sheina was due on Sunday, July 26, 2015.

That day came and went.

By the time we went to our first late visit the following Wednesday, the doctors were getting nervous and asked us to drive down to Provo first thing in the morning to see if we could get an appointment with a specialist.

Dinner was tense that evening.

No one ever wants to hear that their doctor is nervous, and being told you need to wake up early and drive an hour just to roll the dice and potentially get in to see a specialist is not the easiest news to hear, especially for a young couple going through their first pregnancy.

We were nervous, confused, and anxious about the next day.

Yet another situation I couldn't control.

We sat quietly around our kitchen table, doing our best to make small talk and distract ourselves. And then suddenly, Sheina started having contractions.

We called our doula (a fancy name for a labor coach), and she came over and sat with Sheina, who had begun the process of early labor. Our doula explained that it wasn't time to go to the hospital just yet, but we needed to be ready because it could happen at any moment. At one point in the night, she turned to me and said, "You should go get a few hours of sleep because it may be the last night for quite some time you actually get some rest."

Those would prove to be sage words.

I managed to sleep for a few hours, and as morning broke, we were getting close, so we rushed to the hospital. I'll never forget that drive—it was an impossible challenge to drive as fast as humanly possible while also avoiding even the smallest crack in the pavement. All while your laboring wife alternates between howling through her contractions and howling at your driving. As we raced down 1300 East to welcome our first child into the world, our hearts raced even faster.

After we arrived at the hospital, things continued to move quickly. Doctors and nurses surrounded Sheina. This was it. Our lives were about to change forever.

8 cm.

9 cm.

10 cm.

And then, on July 30 at 3:13 p.m., we heard the first cry.

"Why don't you say hello to your son," the nurse said as she put Immanuel into my arms.

My son laid in my arms and looked up, locking eyes with me for the first time. I imagine for most fathers, that's one of the most profound and powerful moments of their lives.

It wrecked me.

I completely crumbled.

This little boy deserved a father who could walk on water, who knew the answer to every possible question a child may ask, and who could accomplish anything and everything in this world.

But no . . . he's getting me.

A lifetime of self-loathing, inadequacy, and shame left me feeling like the furthest possible thing from that reality.

This was not what I expected.

Fatherhood was supposed to be the one thing I could do. The thing that made me whole again. I genuinely thought I would be a good father from the start. If this was my flight of stairs, I was going to sprint up it like Rocky Balboa. But before I even got a chance to try, I already felt like a failure.

This was my last frontier. The last substantive change I had. My ace of spades.

But as I stood there, holding my son in my arms, it hit me.

This isn't going to work. I can't do this. I'm going to let this sweet boy down.

I felt devastated.

Disgusted.

Damaged.

And I felt more loathsome than ever before.

I held my son close and smiled at the squalling little boy, then I handed him back to the nurse as my life crumbled into a million pieces.

The sleepless nights that followed didn't help.

After adding the general exhaustion and chaotic nature of parenting a newborn to all my shame, I quickly became a shell of myself. I turned sullen, withdrawn, and moody.

Marriage wasn't the cure.

Becoming a Rabbi wasn't the cure.

Fatherhood wasn't the cure.

Now I was out of ideas.

A new vicious cycle began to play out in my life. I sat at home and yearned to go to the office to space out. And when I went to the office, I yearned to go home and space out. The next day, I'd do it all over again.

Every day.

On repeat.

My life felt like a scene in a movie where someone gets into an accident and is fading out. All their loved ones are around them screaming, "The ambulance is on its way. Stay with us. Don't go to the dark side." At some point, the patient doesn't hear any siren in the distance and succumbs to the pain.

I had been kidding myself. I had been holding out hope for one change of circumstance after another, knowing deep down that stuff on the outside couldn't do much for the stuff on the inside. But I had fibbed and built myself an illusion, a mistaken sense of security. My sirens weren't coming. The numbness was closing in, and the pain was fading. I had fought so hard for so long.

But I had fought long enough.

I'm done holding on.

13

An Intervention
of Sorts

February 2016

"Avremi, is everything okay?"

That was not what I expected to hear when my parents invited me over for what would become one of the most important conversations I've ever had.

Despite my inner battles, I thought I had everyone tricked. I thought I was keeping up appearances, managing to convince everyone I was okay.

Apparently my acting wasn't good enough.

"We can tell something is bothering you," my mother said. "What's going on?"

"Nothing," I responded, trying to brush it off as every man ever in the history of the world has done in the face of an uncomfortable conversation. "Everything is fine. I'm fine."

I smiled, hoping that would bring some closure to what was shaping up to be an uncomfortable conversation. My siblings and I grew up having deep conversations about God and faith but never really about our emotions. I figured they'd let me off the hook easy.

I was wrong.

"Look, Avremi," my mother continued. "We think it's time for you to go talk to somebody."

"I'm fine. Really. I'm sorry if I'm irritable. Immanuel was up late; I'm just tired."

That part was true. Immanuel wasn't a super easy baby, so I wasn't sleeping much, and when I did, it was for very short stints. But my parents weren't buying it; they knew something else was going on. Something deeper. And they were right.

Fatherhood was the best and worst thing for the depression I was grappling with.

During the pregnancy while we waited for Immanuel, Sheina and I were textbook first-time-parents-to-be. We read every book. We signed up for a painfully long pregnancy class. We fretted over every possible activity.

And we counted.

Days.

Weeks.

Months.

We counted every possible way to look at pregnancy and delighted in the growth from olive to prune to medium strawberry to large strawberry to lime. I even remember driving to the grocery store to see if there was really a difference between medium and large strawberries.

I found solace in the progress.

But when Immanuel was born, something changed. All the finish lines went away. Suddenly, there was no end in sight. There was no progress to mark, no victories to celebrate. We weren't tallying the days. And without a north star to chase, my mental health began to plummet, one miserable day at a time.

"What do you mean talk to someone?" I asked, wondering if it had really come to this. "Like a therapist or something?"

"Yes," my father responded. "One session. That's our ask."

I had less than zero interest in the idea. It wasn't enough that I was feeling so down in the dumps. Now I had to talk about it too? Wouldn't it be far more helpful to just focus my energy on not feeling that way? The way I saw it, therapy was an environment where people came in with issues and spent time talking about said issues. I could not, for the life of me, see value in that. I knew I needed to do whatever possible to cut off vitality from these nothingburgers.

But they weren't going to budge.

As we talked, I realized there was one good thing that could come out of this. I'd been carrying around a question for several years that I'd never vocalized.

Four years earlier, I had fractured my patella in a basketball accident and needed knee surgery. Knee surgery is painful, but it pales in comparison to the torture of being confined to your own bed or couch for the better part of a month.

I just laid there, day after day, letting my body heal.

I figured I may as well make some good use of my time, so during that month, I got a law degree from *Law & Order* University. At the very least, I felt like I was entitled to a degree, given the quantity of episodes I was binging. I watched hours and hours of *Law & Order SVU (Special Victims Unit)*. Every episode of *SVU* tells an action-packed story full of crime, court, prison, and the pain that follows.

I've always enjoyed those episodes. In the moment, I couldn't explain why, but there was always something about that particular spinoff that felt more meaningful than the other series. As episode after episode piled up, one stood out above all the others—Season 12, Episode 23.

The episode is about a fourteen-year-old boy named Hunter who gets into some trouble and seems to be acting out. As the detectives begin to dig, an explanation is eventually revealed for Hunter's behavior. A lady named Ellen, Hunter's old babysitter, had sexually abused him when he was seven years old.

I'll never forget sitting on my couch, rehabbing my knee, wondering if there was a much deeper wound in my life that needed healing.

Did what happened to me "qualify" as sexual abuse?

I have wondered that ever since.

The only thing more awkward than the actual events was the thought of asking someone I knew that question. So instead, I quickly shut it down and swept the pain back under the rug.

When my parents told me I needed to talk to a therapist, I knew enough to know that everything I said would be protected by the law. Maybe this was my chance. Maybe I could make one good thing come out of this hour. I could finally put this question to rest.

I'll ask him, he'll tell me yay or nay, and we can all move on with life.

"Fine," I told them. "I'll go."

14

Therapy

February 2016

Walking into Dr. Michaels's office was exactly what you'd expect.

It looked like a stock photo, as if whoever decorated it had Googled "therapist's office" and copied the first image that popped up.

There was an armchair, a couch, and a giant thermos of coffee. I rolled my eyes when I saw more books than should be legal for a human being to read, titles featuring advice on any topic in the world.

My eye roll only got worse when Dr. Michaels walked in.

He looked like someone had called a male therapist out of central casting. He was in his mid-60s, wore thick glasses that highlighted a gray goatee, a thick sweater, and shoes that suggested a desire to fit into a generation in which he had no place.

Appearances didn't matter. The clock was ticking, and I had one mission. Leaning back on the couch, we exchanged a few pleasantries, and then I went straight for the jugular.

"Look, I think I may have been sexually abused as a kid. By my nanny. For like a while."

In my mind, there were two ways this could go. He could say, "Yup, you have been. Congrats, you're officially a victim of child abuse! You'll never have to own up to any issue in your life again."

Or he could look down on me through those glasses and say, "Come on now, that's nonsense. First off, you're a guy, and that doesn't happen to guys, and from your caregiver? Impossible. You're making excuses. Cut the crap and own up to life."

He said neither.

Instead, he clicked his pen on and off, straightened his glasses, and said, "Tell me more."

And so off we went, and before I knew it, an hour had passed. When I noticed the time, I looked up at him.

"You know what, this wasn't all that bad."

I meant it. Dr. Michaels asked great questions. Questions I never considered asking anyone. I had done what my parents asked me to do, putting in my time and talking to someone. But I found myself wanting to keep going, as if I had more to discover in this office, drenched with cliché as it was.

"So, Dr. Michaels," I began, feeling the weight of a loaded question, "how many more times would you like to see me?"

There was a lot of snark in the question. My innocuous words wanted to ascertain something slightly heavier. I think I assumed all those scribbles he'd made on his notepad led him to a diagnosis—as if he had figured out my problem and was about to plug it into a formula that would spit out my prescription: *Five more sessions ought to do it. Four, if you also read this book.*

That's not what he said, because that's not how the whole therapy thing works.

Instead, he smiled and said, "Why don't you come back next week." His seemingly innocent answer matched my abovementioned question. Easy-enough-to-understand words that belied a far heavier reality.

There's no global roadmap to healing. Come back again and we'll see how the road unfolds before us.

So I did. I went back the next week. And the week after that. And most weeks since.

Dr. Michaels didn't rush me to any conclusions; he didn't tell me I was sexually abused. Instead, he helped me put the evidence on the table and connect the dots. He let me discover that 2 + 2 = 4 on my own.

I slowly realized that so much of the shame I felt came from the things I was asked to do when I was younger. They came from being thrown into a situation I was not ready to handle, a situation I didn't have the maturity to process.

I had never heard the word "grooming" before.

The more we unpacked the years of events, the easier it was to see how Vina took advantage of the ecosystem I was raised in to manipulate me. When she told me she was teaching me how to be a good husband, those weren't just words. They were a weapon, handcrafted with a purpose. Expressed to cater to my desire to lead and please. Uttered to pull me into a trap, a trap that no eight-year-old could ever see coming.

Especially not an eight-year-old who grew up in a house like mine.

She knew my beliefs would keep me trapped. She knew I'd never tell another living soul what was going on. I couldn't. I was too full of shame. It would've gone against every fiber of my being.

So instead, I ran to the only adult I felt safe around: her.

Over and over again.

For ten years.

Over several months, Dr. Michaels helped me discover what had always been true but I had never been able to see. He often quoted Oscar Wilde: "Everything in the world is about sex, with the exception of sex. Sex is about power." The things happening in my downstairs basement were about so much more than my eight-year-old self lacking self-control.

It was about power.

It was about manipulation.

It was about a wounded adult taking advantage of an innocent and confused child.

Up until that point, I was convinced I was the problem. I couldn't comprehend that an adult, especially one I loved and trusted, would manipulate me. I truly believed this was entirely on me.

She was just helping me become a better husband, right? Wasn't she just doing her part to prepare me for my spouse?

All it did was mess me up, throw me into a spiral of depression, and make intimacy with my wife more difficult. But on some level, I still believed her.

That's how deep the lies were ingrained in my mind.

Week by week, self-applied bandages came off. Real wounds were exposed, and for the first time in their existence, they were properly treated. Lies had no place in that office. Excuses weren't tolerated. There was no time for lazy traverses down the road of self-flagellation. Honesty was expected. Sincerity was demanded. Authenticity was the only way forward. And I sure had a lot to learn about those newly discovered skills.

Dr. Michaels helped me understand that no single experience or decision was an isolated incident—no one moment existed in a vacuum.

Learning that was incredibly important, because the most challenging part of the journey was admitting to the shift around age fourteen when my body and my mind started changing. Because the truth is, there were times when I became the one initiating the encounters.

The shame I felt after those days was almost unbearable. It went against everything I believed and everything I valued. It felt like my body was betraying me.

So why did I do it?

As we did the work, I began to see that I had been stuck in a pattern that started when I was eight. Those actions were birthed out of manipulation and abuse.

I had been hurt, harmed, and the victim of a crime. And it wasn't my fault.

I think there's a perception that when survivors go to therapy, they spend a lot of their time re-remembering some of the stuff that happened, almost as if the file had been deleted and the information just needed to be re-added to the hard drive.

That wasn't the case for me.

My traumatic experiences were scratched so deeply onto my mind that they felt like a curse I could never get away from, like a perpetual loop playing on repeat in my brain.

Early therapy wasn't about remembering all the incidents. It was about giving proper perspective to all the experiences I suffered through.

I fought a lot of it at first.

It may sound surprising, but many survivors push back on a lot of the realizations mentioned above. We are hardwired to believe it's almost more acceptable to be guilty than to be taken advantage of.

I didn't want to believe that I had been hurt so badly. I'd rather stew in my sorrow than accept that someone snuck through my defenses and broke me. But after a lot of hard work, I began to understand it all.

I began to understand that Vina never had to make a threat to keep me silent because she knew my beliefs would do the trick.

I began to understand the imbalance of power.

I began to understand why things that were so easy for others to process were so difficult for me.

I began to understand my obsession with the control that was taken away from me at such a young age.

It took some time, but eventually I began to realize the truth.

I am a survivor of sexual abuse.

———

At a certain point, Dr. Michaels started talking about the importance of bringing my inner circle into this conversation. The people who brought on this intervention were about to find out they got a lot more than they bargained for.

Sheina was first.

Dr. Michaels helped me craft a good way to talk through the events with her, but no wordsmith could ever soften the blow. It's hard to express how far beyond the pale of normality this was.

"You could've told me you were an accomplished astronaut who was on his way to Mars before we met," she told me at one point. "And that would've been more plausible than this."

Because "this" doesn't happen in our community.

Her perception of reality was shattered.

Dr. Michaels told me beforehand the most important thing to communicate was that I was aware she would have her own path of healing. I knew that. I understood that. And I told her I supported her process. I also told her I knew her path of healing would sometimes make it difficult to support me in mine and vice versa.

We both left it there.

Hanging between us.

A few weeks later, I had a much different conversation with my parents. Dr. Michaels and I talked through this one repeatedly, because my sole goal was to protect them from the guilt I knew they would feel.

I told them this wasn't their fault, and I stand by my words to this day. I firmly believe there was nothing they could've done to stop Vina from doing what she did. But that's the funny thing about guilt—even when you tell someone not to feel it, they still do.

I went on to tell them the same thing I told Sheina. I knew their path to healing was theirs, and I'd respect that. And so the four of us left that conversation and meandered out into the darkness, each one of us on our own path, gearing up for the lonely journey ahead.

Four people who were going to have to figure out how to heal alone, together.

15

God Must
Hate Me

September 2016

For a very long time, I thought God hated me. I spent a lifetime trying to appease Him. I devoted my life to trying to tip the scales back, to repay God for episode after episode of staring at those roses on the wall of our basement bathroom.

Therapy changed that.

I realized during those sessions that God didn't hate me; He ignored me. On His watch, my innocence was taken. On His watch, my childhood was destroyed. On His watch, my life was ruined.

What kind of God does that?

One day, I walked out of Dr. Michaels's office and realized that God was no longer worthy of my appeasements.

The God I grew up learning about, devoting my life to serving, and making a career out of selling to others was all-knowing, all-seeing, all-capable, and all-powerful. If all that was true, that means God knowingly turned the other way while my life unraveled.

Through therapy, I came to understand that it was easy and more comfortable for me to be the guilty party rather than live in a world where He had so profoundly let me down.

I didn't know what to do with Him.

So I figured I'd let Him know.

———

Around that time, prayer began to take on a very different meaning. Up until that point, I prayed in Hebrew. I'd recite the Hebrew prayers we'd recited for thousands of years. I'd always found a lot of comfort in those prayers—there's solidarity in them, a reminder that you are a part of a much bigger tradition.

But I needed to start praying differently.

I'd be halfway through reading a Hebrew prayer, and then I'd open my eyes, look up to the sky and say, "By the way, God—what the hell?"

That one isn't in the prayer book, but it's what was coming out. Prayer became less about reciting what was in the book and more about communicating what was in my heart.

I found that I shared my feelings best in English.

I needed to communicate using words outside the liturgy of the prayer book.

———

Changing my prayer strategy helped me immensely. It helped me discover how much cognitive dissonance I was living with.

God is all-powerful, and I devoted my life to serving Him, and yet, all I had to show for it was a decade of sexual abuse. Avremi, the flourishing Yeshiva student turned Rabbi, prayed to God with gratitude, thanking Him for His grandiosity. But Avremi, the victim, needed space to speak his piece.

"What gives?"

"What kind of God allows a child to be harmed?"

"Where were you?"

"Where are you?"

Those prayers were incredibly freeing.

They helped me reconcile two very different parts of me, and accept both of them. For years, I tried to silence Avremi the victim so that Avremi the Rabbi could shine, but that wasn't working. It created a dissonance in me that led to endless hours of scrolling through ESPN.

Therapy helped me see another option. I could give Avremi the victim the microphone and let him ask God all the questions he held on to for years.

When I let the questions fly, I realized that was okay.

Maybe God could handle my honesty.

Maybe God was big enough for my questions.

Maybe God didn't need me to have all the answers all the time.

Because maybe, just maybe, wrestling with God is part of the journey.

———

A few years ago, my cousin lost a beautiful little girl to an aggressive form of pediatric cancer.

In my line of work, I'm sadly no stranger to pain and suffering. I've been asked all the questions there are to ask about God's decision-making:

Why would God . . . ?

What kind of God would . . . ?

Where was God when . . . ?

When will God stop . . . ?

At some point, I figured it was only fitting for me to stand alongside the legions of those enduring pain and suffering and add my questions to the ever-growing heap. Because expecting them to be answered in some form is truly not what I signed up for. Not what I'm expecting in the least. If God needed to show me or prove to me or justify for me each of His actions, then I'd apply for His job. Such is not the nature of our relationship.

At a certain point, I figured it was wiser to stop wondering why He did it to me, and instead try to figure out what He intended for me to do with it.

I needed to stop asking "*why* me?" and start asking "why *me*?"

Is there some sort of purpose that could come about through my pain?

Would that make it worth it?

16

The Spark

Summer 2017

"Happy Birthday!"

Facebook is a place where it's easy to lose track of time, mindlessly scrolling without really registering what you are looking at. But every once in a while you'll see something so infuriating that it snaps you out of your unconscious scrolling.

A seemingly innocent "Happy Birthday!" followed by hearts and smile emojis. Forty-five million people send birthday wishes on Facebook every single day, so why was this one so different for me?

This one was from the Facebook account of "Rodger Alavina Florreich" to a young man in our neighborhood.

I sat at my kitchen table and glared at that message, realizing for the first time that this whole thing may be bigger than just Vina and me. Were there other victims? Were there other soon-to-be victims?

Messing with me is one thing, but the thought of her repeating her abuse with other kids sparked something deep in my soul—the start of a fire that would not be extinguished without a fight.

"She's still doing it!" I blurted out, storming into Dr. Michaels's office. I'm not sure what he had planned for our session that day, but he threw all that out when he heard the tone in my voice. True to form, he didn't react to my emotions; instead, he calmly responded with a question.

"Doing what?"

"Look," I vented, throwing the phone into his hand to show him the birthday post. "Do you know what this means?"

He probably knew exactly where I was going, but he let me say it.

"It means she's still doing it. She's still trying to convince the rest of the world that she was trying to make little boys into good husbands."

Dr. Michaels nodded in understanding. And like any good therapist, he didn't tell me what to do. Instead, he asked me questions that helped me navigate my anger and think through a way to respond.

The more we talked, the more anxious I got. My hands began to sweat, my chest tightened, and my breaths became short and shallow. The deep passion I felt to advocate for others was at war with the shame and fear I felt about telling my story publicly.

I was just beginning to formulate language for what was happening inside me at the time. Months earlier, we had a conversation steered in the direction of CPTSD (complex post-traumatic stress disorder). The first mention of PTSD got a full-blown snort from me.

Me and the guy from American Sniper? *What do we have in common? I have PTSD? And I didn't even have to sleep on the ground or risk my life for it?*

Dr. Michaels was pivotal in slowing the conversation down and helping to remove the stigma from the topic. Yes, the common carriers of PTSD are soldiers in war zones and cops in gang units. But let's face it. When you go through dozens of highly charged, profoundly traumatic experiences at a young age, it'll affect how you handle stress. One might even say it can cause a problem for you in the long term that needs to be treated adequately.

A disorder.

All told, I came to accept the CPTSD and began to work on a way to regulate it. I used to joke about my "C." Some people get regular PTSD. I found a great deal online and managed to get CPTSD for the same price.

The jokes were just my way of coping with the weight of it.

The reality is that the "C" is typically associated with repeated trauma. All PTSD is complex, but when the thing causing the trauma was repeated over an extended period of time (like ten years of sexual abuse), it adds another layer of complexity.

I would later begin to understand that CPTSD was one of several reasons any thought of talking about the abuse publicly made my chest tighten and my breath speed up. At the time, I wasn't ready to go there, so my response was quick and straightforward. I told Dr. Michaels the same thing I'd told him a million times.

"I can't report her," I said. "Reporting her would mean going public. And being a survivor of childhood sexual abuse in my community is a nonstarter."

Let me try to unpack those sentences.

In my mind at the time, the moment a private citizen calls up their local law enforcement and files a police report, that report becomes a matter of public record. If I reported what Vina had done to me, people would know. The public would know. Everyone would know.

I was less concerned about the folks there in Salt Lake City and more about how this would land in the wider religious community. I would be connecting myself to a topic that just wasn't discussed in our circles. It just didn't happen. One could make the argument that it didn't happen because it wasn't discussed. I would be giving oxygen and airtime to the most taboo of taboo topics.

More than anything, I'd be admitting that I had a problem. That I struggled with something.

In our community, we love people with problems. They're what allow us to do good deeds, and in all fairness, we excel at doing good deeds. If there was a young person in Timbuktu who was a survivor of child sexual abuse and they needed to be rescued at tremendous cost and sacrifice, we'd do it. In a heartbeat. Every day and twice on Sunday. The more people with problems that you help, the more you rise to prominence in the community. But there's a careful distinction to be mindful of. You can help folks that have them, but God forbid you or someone close to you has those problems. The buck stops with us. The more complicated your life might seem, the more we'll classify you as troubled and lend a hand. The further you move from the "troubled" status, the higher on the pedestal you can go.

I'm not ready.

He understood the weight in my words. And although we could both sense the unsettling feeling that hung in the air and the cognitive dissonance I was wrestling with, he wisely reminded me that he understood.

We kept the rest of the conversation light and didn't put any pressure on ourselves to make any decisions that day.

As our session ended, I thanked him and got up to leave. But this time, as I walked out, something was different.

Where there was once an emptiness, a hollowness, something had changed.

Something was moving.

Something was shaking.

There may not have been a fire in my heart yet, but there was a spark.

17

Aly

January 18, 2018

I'm a sports nut.

It doesn't matter what the sport is; if two humans are competing and there's going to be a winner and a loser, I'm hooked. I want to watch it, learn from it, and understand it.

I was in London for Yeshiva in 2012, and although I didn't attend any Olympic events, the city was swept up in Olympic fever. It so fondly reminded me of Salt Lake City in 2002. Usain Bolt outran everyone on the track. USA Basketball seemed like they started every game with a 50-point lead. And the USA Women's Gymnastics team dominated the gym.

Aly Raisman was a key piece of that team. And more than my patriotic connections, she was proudly Jewish and performed her gold medal routine on the floor to "Hava Nagila." I was a fan.

Something else happened in the sports world in 2012, and at the time, it had no visible connection to Aly. The Penn State football scandal reached a boiling point, and Jerry Sandusky was sentenced to prison and charged with fifty-two counts of sexual abuse of young boys over fifteen years.

Even though this was 2012, years before I went to therapy and started sorting through my abuse, I was still fascinated by the story. I consumed every possible piece of press. And as was so often the case, the story was all about Sandusky's actions and Joe Paterno conspiring with him.

It was all about the bad guys.

The perpetrators.

The cover-uppers.

But the victims?

They were usually relegated to a brief line in the fourth or fifth paragraph, where it would describe nameless, faceless, hurt creatures who had been raped and sodomized in a locker room shower. The line usually said something about how they only took part in the camps because they came from broken homes, reinforcing every stereotype imaginable about victims being weak and defenseless.

As a human being, your heart breaks for these poor kids. And yet, at the same time, there seems to be a clear message about what sort of people wear the title of "survivor of child sexual abuse." Kids from broken homes. Troubled young people, marginalized by society in every imaginable way. Nameless and faceless and cowering in fear. Not the sort of fraternity you'd want to be lumped in with.

Then 2017 arrived, and another sexual abuse scandal rocked the sports world.

It came out that Larry Nassar, a USA Gymnastics doctor, had abused a staggering number of girls. The ignorance and the cover-ups were atrocious. So many people failed the victims. But this one was different. It wasn't Nassar's face you saw everywhere.

It was Aly Raisman's face.

It was Jordyn Wieber's face.

It was Jamie Dantzscher's face.

And it was so many other strong, defiant survivors. They weren't faceless beings; they were out there, in public, reclaiming their voice.

Suddenly being a survivor didn't feel so lonely anymore.

———

January 18, 2018, was a slow day at the office, but it became memorable for one reason.

I had a lot on my mind and was scrolling through ESPN, looking for a bit of escape, when I came across the video of Aly's impact statement at the Nassar sentencing. I clicked it out of curiosity and had no idea how transformative the next twelve minutes and forty-nine seconds would be.

I'll never forget Aly's bright blazing pink jacket; it was fitting for the fiery statements she was delivering. "Larry, you do realize now that we, this group of women you so heartlessly abused over such a long period of time, are now a force, and you are nothing."

She stood five feet away from her abuser, calling him by name and looking him dead in the eye. No fear. No mercy. No balancing statements.

"Larry, you abused the power and trust I and so many others placed in you, and I am not sure I will ever come to terms with how horribly you manipulated and violated me."

Part of me wanted to avert my eyes, click the X, and stop watching. But I couldn't look away. How could someone do that? How could someone find the strength to say those things out loud, on national television, with their abuser right in front of them?

I couldn't bring myself to watch it. Stronger than that, I couldn't bring myself to stop watching it.

The honesty was searing.

The pain was palpable.

It was exhilarating.

And terrifying.

And inspiring.

As I watched, the spark in my heart was beginning to spread.

18

The Marathon

January 28, 2018

I looked up at the clock.

Five hours and forty-two minutes.

Not the time I expected, but I couldn't care less.

I had gone from being a couch potato to running 26.2 miles in two years. Who cared if my time resembled wet cement?

During one of our first sessions, Dr. Michaels recommended that I start exercising. It didn't matter what it was, but he told me I needed a physical outlet. Processing the trauma was going to be an intense experience, so endorphins would be my friend.

Running seemed like the right move.

So I bought a new pair of shoes, set my alarm, and ran about halfway down my block on day one before I felt like I was going to pass out. You know the expression "you've got to learn to walk before you can run"? Turns out, it's some pretty sage advice on the most basic of levels.

Taking nice, long walks became part of my daily routine. After a few weeks, I'd jog the last block of the way home. Months later, I was able to jog most of the way, then all of the way.

Eventually I worked my way up to a 5K. And then a 10K.

A friend of mine from my Yeshiva days had recently undergone a huge weight-loss program, culminating with running the Miami Half Marathon in January 2016.

If he can, I thought, *I can do it.*

January of 2017, just about a year into therapy, I flew down to Florida and completed the Miami Half Marathon. Crossing that finish line was great but felt incomplete. My ever-competitive nature did not like sufficing with half measures of any kind. So I promised myself I'd be back next year for the full.

I did all the things over that year—watching what I ate, entering a comprehensive training program, and above all, promising myself I'd get it done.

I got through the first thirteen miles of the Miami Marathon pretty well. A friend of mine who was also in the Full was running at about my speed, and we knocked out thirteen miles step for step. In Miami, the crowds are deep all along the route for the Half, cheering you on. Once you make the turn for the Full, they literally disappear. You don't know what you've got until it's gone. Without the crowd you realize just how much you were relying on their support.

At about 15.5 miles, I was cramping and gave in to a bathroom break. I broke the cardinal rule of long-distance running: I stopped moving. Starting up again was brutal.

With a mixture of walking, plodding, and some light jogging, five hours and forty-two minutes later, I completed the Full.

As proud as I was of my accomplishment, I also decided God did not have 26.2 miles in mind for someone still recovering from knee surgery. I knew this was going to be it for me—one and done. So I made the most of it. I took all the cheesy photographs. Wearing the medal. Kissing the medal. Biting the medal. All of it.

And I shared them online.

A few minutes later, I received a text from my friend Craig who had seen my post and invited me to grab lunch the next day on my way to the airport. Craig was a lawyer who lived in Salt Lake City but did a lot of work in Miami, and he happened to be out there. We had always wanted to get together in Utah but had never been able to because there weren't any Kosher restaurants. But there were in Miami.

I was excited to spend some time with Craig because I'd always loved the law. And I don't just mean episodes of *Law and Order*. I've always been fascinated by the entire judicial system.

Craig is the kind of guy who always has a story and whose stories inevitably beget other stories. For the first thirty minutes of the meal, I sat back and listened to all his latest escapades. But during one story, he referenced his years right out of law school and offhandedly mentioned that he had spent some years serving as a deputy prosecutor.

I didn't hear a word he said after that.

In the aftermath of the events of the preceding months, spanning from the Facebook birthday post and ending in Aly's impact statement, the fire that burned within me to report was as aflame as ever. But I still wasn't sure I was ready for it all to be public information, and I figured if I called the cops, the story would be out there for anyone with an iPhone and a little Wi-Fi to access.

Seeing as I was only going off my own ignorant speculations about the legal system, Dr. Michaels had advised me to seek the advice of someone who actually knew the system from the inside. A cop, prosecutor, former, present—whatever it may be. He suggested finding someone who could provide definitive answers to these questions.

A few days after Dr. Michaels suggested this, I flew to Miami to run a marathon because he had encouraged me to start exercising two years earlier. I posted about it because I was so proud. And before I knew it, I found myself sitting across the table from a former prosecutor.

That didn't feel like a coincidence.

"Hey Craig, I've got a question for you. I've got this friend . . ."

This is a perk of being a clergy member. You can invent any sort of member of your congregation and make all your problems belong to them. I told Craig about my fictional friend who was anxious to report his abuse to the police because police reports are public knowledge, then I asked if he had any advice.

"Yeah, that's totally ridiculous," he said as he popped a French fry into his mouth. "On no planet are police reports a part of public record. It would have to become a full-on investigation for that to happen. Tell your friend he's a moron."

I took a sip of my beer, smiled, and told my friend he was a moron.

19

You Can Call
Me Brian

January 30, 2018

Call? Or don't call?

I put my phone back on my desk for the hundredth time and tried to get back to work. But focusing on the things happening at the synagogue was next to impossible. I couldn't stop glancing back at the phone doing cartwheels on my desk. My mind raced.

Call? Or don't call?

How does one even go about reporting a crime that happened over a decade ago? I didn't want to call 911 and interrupt any real emergencies, but was there another option? It's funny how much you don't know about life until you get thrown into situations. After a quick Google search, I learned there was a non-emergency number I knew nothing about, presumably for such a time as this.

Call? Or don't call?

I'm not sure if it was a moment of intense weakness or inner strength, but I decided the discomfort of being on the fence was worse than anything that could come from the phone call, so I grabbed my coat, climbed the stairs up out of my office, and went outside.

"Salt Lake City Police Department," the operator said. "Can I help you?"

I froze.

What in God's name was I supposed to say? *Yes, hi, how are you? I want to report a crime that happened a long time ago.*

I'll forever be grateful for the patience of the operator who answered the phone that morning. I'm sure I wasn't the first person to draw a blank; she just went with it as I did my best to explain something I had only ever told my therapist and family.

The conversation lasted all of five minutes, and everything I told her was very general.

"I'm going to have an officer call you in a few minutes. Can you sit tight and hang by the phone?"

An officer? Like a real one?

"Yeah, okay," I said. "Thanks."

"No problem. Can I take down your name, hun?"

Out of all the questions she asked, that should've been the easiest— the softball lobbed over the plate. Instead, it made me shake.

My "friend" I had told Craig about wasn't ready for the world to know. "Do I have to give you a real name?" I asked her.

"Nope."

Perfect.

"Well, then you can call me Brian."

Brian? Really? Out of all the names out there, I went with Brian?

I'll never know where that name came from.

Sure enough, three minutes later, "Brian" got a call.

"Hello, this is Officer Stone from SLC Police Department. I've got a couple of questions for you today, Brian."

In for a penny, in for a pound. I brought this on myself, so I guessed I had to answer the man's questions. As he began to probe, I realized this round was way more specific.

"What's her name? Where does she live? Is she still working for any family? Have you told anyone else?"

I suppose my answers were sufficient because he wrapped up the call by telling me he would send my case to a detective at sex crimes. "You should be hearing from them soon."

I hated myself for asking, but I did anyway, "Okay, great. But what does 'pretty soon' mean?"

"If you don't hear from him in forty-eight hours, give us a call. I've got a case number for you, if you wanna write it down."

Case number? Now I have a case number? Who am I, James Bond?

After I took down all the information on my phone, the moment of truth came.

"If we are going to move forward from here, I am going to need your real name."

I swallowed hard and took a deep breath.

"Avrohom," I said. "My name is Avrohom Zippel."

Then I went back inside and laughed. It felt like a fun lunch activity. But I knew the odds of anything coming from that phone call were slim to none.

I don't ever play the Powerball. Being raised in Utah where there is no lottery made the whole concept seem unappealing. But I couldn't help thinking back to the one time I did.

I was in New Jersey at the time when a couple of friends and I found out the Powerball was over 700 million dollars. We started dreaming about everything we'd do with that money and dutifully went down to 7-Eleven to buy our tickets.

There is a moment at that counter, as your ticket is being printed, when you actually believe you have a shot. But when we got back into our car, reality set in, and we began to laugh at the idiocy of what we had just done.

Talking to the officer on the phone felt a lot like that. I appreciated the police department's patience, and I was grateful they humored me and allowed me to buy my Powerball ticket. But now it was back to the real world.

———

On Thursday, my phone rang. It was a 385 number I didn't recognize.

"Good morning. Is this AV-RO-HOM?" said a man who clearly practiced that too many times.

"Yes, it is."

"I'm Detective Kevin Blue. I'm an officer in sex crimes at SLCPD, and your case file made it across my desk."

I gulped.

Are we actually doing this?

"I'm sorry for all you've been through. I'm wondering if you'd be up for heading down to the station to talk. Just wanna ask you a couple of questions."

A police officer just wants to ask me a couple of questions. My life had become a TV show.

The situation suddenly started to feel a bit too real. I wanted to report because I was angry. I wanted to report to check a box and do my part. But I wasn't ever crazy enough to believe this was possible.

Even after two full years of therapy, I still carried around so much shame from that decade of abuse that the prospect of "heading down to the station to talk" seemed way too daunting.

I trusted Sheina.

I trusted my parents.

I trusted Dr. Michaels.

But the cops? A detective I'd never met? It sounded like this guy had a code name, for crying out loud. Detective Blue? Are there really human beings with Blue for a last name?

However, I had come this far. So against my better judgment, I agreed.

On Wednesday, February 7, at 1 p.m., I headed downtown to talk to a sex crimes officer named Detective Blue.

What could possibly go wrong?

20

Detective Blue

February 7, 2018.

"Idiot. Idiot. Idiot."

There wasn't a whole lot of positive self-talk going on as I drove downtown. Instead, I pounded the steering wheel and considered turning around a hundred times.

I had been inside the Public Safety Building several times. We often took the kids from our community there during summer camp to hang up "Thank You, Officers" signs on the doors and hand out cookies to the friendly men and women who were perfect strangers to all of us.

This was not that.

This couldn't be more different from that.

Now I was heading in to meet with a detective. How was I even supposed to "check in"? Should I knock on the bulletproof glass and say, "Yeah, hello, I'm here to meet with a detective who works in SEX CRIMES. His code name is Blue."

I could imagine the conversation.

"And what's your name, sir?"

"I'd rather not tell you," I would say.

"Aha, got it. And what's this about?"

"That I am for sure not telling you."

"Wonderful. The secret agent will be right down."

I'd participated in some dumb activities over the years, but this was at the top of the list. I was about to meet with someone I didn't even know to talk about something I wasn't even sure I was ready to talk about.

I parked in a spot on 500 South and approached the building, my heart pounding. I decided to loiter suspiciously outside for a few minutes so I wouldn't be early. Then at 1 p.m. sharp, I made my move.

A warm blast of air hit me in the face as I opened the door, and an officer came out from behind the desk, looked right at me, and mouthed, "Avrohom?"

I nodded, and we walked inside one of the very doors we'd hung a thank-you poster on seven months prior.

Back in simpler times.

Back when police were people I didn't know.

Not anymore.

Now I was a part of a police investigation.

Nothing about the room was comfortable or inviting. It was cold, dark, and intimidating. The chair was firm, small, and clearly not designed for a friendly chat over coffee. Detective Blue, however, was the opposite of the room.

If Dr. Michaels shouted "Therapist," this guy screamed "Cop."

There's a joke that you can see the cop on someone from a mile away, and Kevin Blue was crafted by Heaven to be a police officer—the haircut, the build, the eyes, the mannerisms. He even had a beat-up notepad (of course he did). I felt like I was in an episode of *Law & Order* and was ready for Christopher Meloni to open the door behind him and ask Detective Blue if he wanted a coffee from a bodega.

Blue's warm, inviting presence made me comfortable enough to level with him.

"Look, I'm going to be honest with you. I want to do this, I really do. But there's a part of me that is certain that at some point during this chat, you're going to walk around to my side of the table and slap the cuffs on me because of what I'm about to tell you."

"Ya know what," he said without skipping a beat. "Let's see where this takes us. You start talking and then call it quits if at some point this doesn't feel safe."

That's what I needed to hear. It may have sounded like textbook cop talk, but hey, he was my textbook cop. So off we went.

He was fantastic.

He asked but didn't push.

Clarified details but didn't probe.

Eventually, I began to tell him about the first few episodes, and for a while, we sufficed with euphemisms, but as the episodes got progressively darker, he finally said it.

"Look, man, I know this can't be easy, but just once, I'm going to need you to specify where she touched you and where she made you touch her. Just once, and we'll get it out of the way."

The pain in his eyes when saying that made him look like he was knowingly breaking the first rule of some unspoken bro code, but a job is a job. So I came out and said it.

"Penis."

I winced but took a deep breath and found my footing again.

That was a huge milestone. With all my disclosures in therapy, Dr. Michaels had sufficed with vague references. She touched me and made me touch her. Let your worst thoughts do the work. I had never had to say it clearly until now, and it was done.

And I was thankful to move on.

We ended up talking for an hour and forty minutes. The direction of the questions at the end was pretty clear.

There were no eyewitnesses.

No corroborating allegations.

No physical evidence.

Just a boatload of traumatic memories. And my word against hers.

At the end of our conversation, he looked over at me with what I felt was a real pain in his eyes. "I want you to know something. I believe you.

I believe every word you just came in here and told me. I really do, man. I'm sorry. And I think you're really brave for doing this."

Then he made his pitch.

"Given what we have, here's what I can promise. Someone will go down to Arizona and talk to Alavina about our conversation. She'll know we talked today. She'll have the ability to disagree with whatever you've said and deny it outright, and if she does . . ."

His voice trailed off into the intricacies of what would happen with the process if she denied it. The rest meant nothing to me. It was one of the most vindicating moments of my life—it felt like justice. He told me that he believed me.

Because of our conversation in this cold, dark room, he was going to go and do something. That's all I wanted. Let a guy with a badge and gun tell Vina that the game was over and that I finally knew what was what.

He believed me. The rest didn't matter.

Detective Blue was careful to mention that these things take time. There's a backlog of cases. Hoops to jump through. Sergeants who need to lend approval. Forty-eight-hour timelines were a thing of the past. This would happen when it happened, and he'd let me know when it did.

After he shook my hand and I got up to leave, I felt lighter than I had in years. But I had one burning question left to ask him.

"Is Blue really your last name? I mean, your given last name? Like your father before you and his father before him?"

"Yeah," he laughed. "Long story. Another time maybe."

———

My phone had been off during the interview, so as I walked back out to a cold, wintry afternoon, I noticed several missed calls from Sheina. In neither of our minds was this going to take close to two hours. I needed a deep steadying breath before I dialed. There was something settling inside me that I was slowly finding words for. It filled me with hope.

Promise. Something to look forward to. A new friend that I'd come to know who went by the name Justice.

"How'd it go?" she asked eagerly the moment she picked up.

"Let me put it this way. If I die today, I'll die a happy man," I provided in place of an answer. "She'll know that she did something wrong to me and the jig is up."

A few days later, I found myself recounting the events to Dr. Michaels. I harped on what it felt like to hear this newfound pal of mine tell me that he believed me.

"I can't even describe what that's like, to hear those words from someone for the first time, for someone to tell me that they believe me, after all the time I've spent denying that truth to myself," I told him.

"I've known you for two years, and I believe you," he came back at me, peering over his plastic lenses.

"Dr. Michaels, I pay you to believe me. I could've told you I know the nuclear codes, and you would have nodded wisely and asked how that made me feel."

It was just witty banter, but there was a lot of truth there for me. Hearing those words from a stranger had gone such a long way. I began to wonder to myself, both silently and aloud, what it would mean to share what had happened to me with other strangers and see how they reacted.

21

Now Do You Believe Me?

March 26, 2018

The week leading up to Passover is always stressful, but 2018 took it to a whole different level.

Back before Covid, it was common for the local TV stations to invite us to their studios before each Jewish holiday to give their viewers a taste of Judaism. I had been invited to FOX 13 that Monday, which meant my day started with a very early sunrise drive to the west side of Salt Lake City.

When you have young kids at home, you learn to relish the car rides you take by yourself. It was a rare window of silence, and I used it to gather my thoughts.

After a little arithmetic in my head, I calculated that it had been seven and a half weeks since my conversation with Detective Blue. So far, I hadn't heard a peep from him or anyone at the department—almost two months of silence.

Which was expected. I was determined not to push any of this.

Honestly, the whole thing still felt mythical, as if I dreamed up that entire conversation I had with him.

And yet, I'd be lying to myself if I said I wasn't curious.

We were scheduled to travel to California on Thursday to spend the holiday with Sheina's parents, which would put us right at the eight-week mark and felt like a fair amount of time to wait. I promised myself I'd shoot him an email if I hadn't heard from him by then.

I never had the chance to send that email. My phone rang before I reached the city.

"Hello?"

"Avrohom, Detective Blue from the SLC Police Department. How are you?"

"I'm good, thanks," I responded, as I squeezed the steering wheel nervously.

"Just wanted to let you know that I got pulled away from your case for a few weeks, but it is now my main focus."

"Great," I said, unsure how to respond. "So what do we do?"

"Well, in cases like these, the best place to start is with a pretextual phone call between you and her. How does that sound?"

"You mean you want me to call her and have a conversation?"

"Yeah." He sounded as if this was a completely normal request. "We'll be recording it, and you'll see if you can get her talking. What do you think?"

What do I think?

How would you get her number?

Why would she answer the phone?

What would I say?

My mind flashed back to that 7-Eleven in New Jersey, to the cashier handing me a Powerball ticket and wishing me luck. His question didn't inspire a whole lot of confidence in the police department.

"I mean, I guess so," I said. "Can't hurt, right?"

"That's the spirit," Detective Blue said in an enthusiastic tone. "How about tomorrow at 10:30?"

My mind was spinning. There were so many logistics we needed to figure out. "Wait, so I'm just supposed to bring up the events? We haven't talked in years. What should I say?"

"I'll leave that up to you, Avrohom. Maybe just tell her you are in counseling and are trying to process through some of the pain."

On its face, that sounded sensible, but painful flashbacks shot that down. The more I thought about it, I kept coming back to her mantra: "This is all to make you a better husband one day."

The abuse continued for years because of one reason: it was just her and me. The only shot I had at getting her to talk was to bring us both back to that space. As much as I would hate myself, I had to allow myself to revisit those moments between us—no talk of the pain, CPTSD, or therapy. On some level she saw herself as my confidant and most trusted ally, and it was in that warped version of reality that we would be able to talk like I was a kid all over again.

As terrible as it would be, the focus had to be on the experiences we shared.

"Detective, I have an idea, but here's a weird question. Am I allowed to lie?"

That's a strange question to ask anyone, let alone a detective.

"Absolutely," he said. "Utah is a one-party consent state. The Supreme Court has ruled unequivocally that you can say what you want on the phone in states like Utah, and how she answers is her problem."

The basis of a plan began to formulate.

"Okay, I have an idea. Thanks, Detective. I'll see you tomorrow."

———

When I got home that evening, I shared the news with Sheina.

"Are you nervous?" she asked. The seriousness of her reaction surprised me.

"Nervous? This is the dumbest idea in the history of the world. It's never going to work. Why would I be nervous?"

The more we talked, the more the reality began to set in that tomorrow could be the day.

"Do you know what's wild?" I said, turning to her. "They said this whole process could take months and months, but this whole investigation could kind of be over tomorrow."

"Ha," she said, the thought beginning to sink in for her as well. "Crazy."

"Ha," I agreed with a smile. "Crazy."

———

Tuesday, March 27 was a special day on the Chabad calendar. That morning, I awoke early to say my prayers and do the various activities to mark the significance of the day, then I headed downtown.

At 10:30 a.m. sharp, Detective Blue was waiting for me in the lobby of the Public Safety Building. We headed through the secure officers' entrance, into a massive elevator, up two stories, and into a part of the building I had never been to before.

"How you feeling?" he asked as the elevator rose.

"Good, I guess. Kind of incredulous at this whole idea."

He looked back with a smile. "Yeah, well, I'm glad you have managed your expectations."

We went into a room on the second floor that was only slightly less intimidating than the one on the main floor I'd been in nearly two months earlier. A second detective was in the room and invited me to sit at the table where a printed handout waited for me. The sheet had Vina's home phone number and a list of talking points they wanted me to try to hit during the call. The goal was clear. They were hoping for a non-denial. Recount the episodes, and if she doesn't flatly deny that they happened, we're in business.

Seemed simple enough.

The three of us talked through it for a couple of minutes, and then the moment arrived. "Alright, let's do it," Detective Blue said, turning on a recorder. "Today is Tuesday, March 27, 2018. It is 1035 hours; I am here with Avrohom Zippel, and we are calling . . ." Then he nodded.

I dialed the number.

Pressed the green call button.

And put it on speaker.

Ring . . . *Well, I guess we're really doing this.*

Ring . . . *No turning back now.*

Ring . . . *How do we know this is the right number?*

Ring . . . *How did we even get this number?*

Ring . . . *When's the last time I even talked to her?*

Ring . . . *What am I doing?*

After the sixth ring, the call went to voicemail. I looked over at Detective Blue, and he motioned at me to kill it. No use leaving a message.

The finality and stupidity of the project arrived packaged together as one.

This was a moronic idea that never had any better than a zero percent chance at success, and that is exactly what we encountered. But hey, if we all had stupid ideas, I figured I'd offer one more.

"Would it be okay to Facebook message her and ask for her number?"

The detectives glanced at each other, shrugged, and then looked back at me, "Yeah, sure," Detective Blue said. "Why not?"

So I typed out a message.

> *Hey Vina! Long, long time! Wanted to chat if you had a minute. What's a good number to reach you at?*

I sent the message, and then we sat around and made small talk for the next few minutes, waiting to see if we'd get a quick response. But there is only so long you can wait. I had a lot to do that day, and I was sure they did too.

"Alright, well, you go have a great day," Detective Blue said. "If you hear from her, you just let us know."

I would not describe myself as dejected as we took the elevator back down to the lobby. Dejected implies there were expectations that this would somehow lead to something, but the prospect had never crossed my mind.

Since I had to pick up a document at City Hall on my way home, I climbed back in my car and headed one block down the street, smiling at how quickly I shifted from being a part of an official police investigation to normal life. The demands of my busy pre-Passover day quickly flushed any thoughts of what would've been if she had answered the phone.

After heading into City Hall and climbing two flights of stairs to the Mayor's office, I retrieved the document and was walking out into the courtyard when my phone buzzed. I had a Facebook message. It was Vina. She had sent me her number. My hand was shaking so violently that I'm not even sure how I managed to call Detective Blue.

"What's up?" he said.

"She wrote me back."

"She did?"

"Yeah!"

"Get back here," Detective Blue shouted. "Quickly."

I dashed to my car, backed it out of the spot, and rushed back to the Public Safety Building. It took me a few moments to register that 500 South was a one-way street and that I couldn't go back the way I came.

Without a moment's consideration for what may have been, I put my car in reverse and backed up about 200 feet to reclaim my parking spot, miraculously avoiding the loss of life and limb of any pedestrians in the process.

I threw my car in park, got out, and sprinted up 500 South, weaving past the library, through a homeless encampment, and into the doors of the Public Safety Building.

Detective Blue was there waiting, anticipation on his face. "Let's go."

We headed back up the elevator to the same room, with the same recorder, and the same copy sheet, with the same talking points.

This time there was no small talk.

"Today's date is March 27, 2018." Detective Blue's voice was clear and concise. "It's approximately 1110 hours. Detective Blue, Salt Lake City Police. We're going to be trying to call Vina at . . ."

He nodded, and I typed in the new number and hit the green button.

Ring . . .

Ring . . .

"Hello?"

My world stopped.

For two years in therapy, I had sat with Dr. Michaels, talking about an almost mythical monster. A person so deeply entrenched in my past, who had affected every facet of my life to that point. But never for a moment had I considered the possibility the day would come when she would transition back from the past and into the present.

The moment was here. But this was no time for nostalgia.

I was a man; this was a mission.

I have to do this.

"Hi . . . Vina?"

"Hello!"

"Hey. How are you? It's been a long time."

"I know."

In all of the great many plans that had gone into this call, I never considered how to make small talk. How does one casually schmooze with the person they've come to understand completely wrecked every facet of their childhood?

The conversation was painful, awkward, and forced. It spun itself in circles for the first eight minutes, going nowhere. I admired the patience of the two detectives sitting next to me. She asked about my brother's diabetes three times. I tried to tell her how old my kids were three times. By then, the disappointment began setting in.

A few moments into the conversation, she called me by name. Ahvrami. She had never gotten my name down when I was a kid, and I had come to accept her adaptation of my name as we all had.

Something changed within me when she said it. I saw her. I smelled her. I heard her say my name a thousand times in the basement bathroom and tell me what a good husband I'd be one day. I needed to fight on.

Somehow I had managed to get to this point. I had a glimmer of hope. But alas, there was no way this conversation was going where we needed it to.

She didn't sound lucid.

I was getting impatient, and so were the detectives. It was time to either put up or shut up.

"Hey, I'm calling because I wanted to talk to you about something. Remember how you met my wife, Sheina, at Sarah's Bat Mitzvah?"

"Sure."

"Well, things have been kind of rough for the two of us."

"Avremi," she responded, the tone in her voice shifting. "I'd be happy to meet up and talk with you."

Um, what now?

There wasn't a chance I was going to attempt this conversation in person. I needed a plausible explanation why it had to happen by phone.

"Well, I'm actually in my car, on the way to Provo, to deliver something to someone before Passover," I said, sensing this was my window. "I was hoping we could talk now?"

"Okay, Rami. Let me close the door because my grandkids are in the other room."

"Sure."

The detectives sat up straight in their chairs and exchanged interested glances. This was on. There was a clear moment of recognition that a conversation was to unfold that shouldn't happen in the presence of children. I steeled myself on the talking points before me, taking every last emotion threatening to flood me at the moment and locking them in a cage. The pain and shrapnel would have to wait. I'd unpack it with Dr. Michaels another day. Today was about justice.

The goal of the conversation was a non-denial. That's it. That's all we were looking for. I looked at the first episode on Detective Blue's list and gently lobbed it in the air, wondering how it might land.

She didn't deny it. Instead, she laughed. "Oh yes," she exclaimed, adding a detail to the episode that I hadn't even brought up.

One episode.

And then another.

And another.

It was important I hang on to these memories, she insisted. These memories would indeed make me a better husband, she implored. I silently sent a prayer Heavenward, thanking God for having sent me someone like Sheina, who picked up the pieces of the wreckage of this monster, someone who truly had made me a better husband.

Detectives working in sex crimes have seen everything. You never want to be the person who surprises the people who have seen it all, but that's exactly what was happening across the table. As I burned through the talking points, Detective Blue frantically searched for more paper to give me ways to keep the conversation going and then start winding it down to an exit.

Then we truly struck gold.

Throughout the interview, one word seemed to spell doom whenever mentioned: Arizona. The fact that she was currently out of state complicated things. And then a gift from on High. She let slip that although I had dialed her Arizona area code, she was currently visiting family for spring break. Right here in Salt Lake City. Under the jurisdiction of the Salt Lake City Police Department. Detective Blue furiously scribbled a new mission on the paper.

Get an address.

I'd get an address, alright, but I had one final question before I did. One unsettled conundrum I needed to bring up.

"Hey Vina, do you ever regret everything we did?"

"No," she quickly answered. "You know, with those memories, I am able to be with Rodger to this day."

I needed to throw up.

Until that moment, I remained calm and collected, with all the emotions and memories locked tightly and securely in a cage. But that line shifted everything. It rallied years of trauma to break free and shatter the cage I had locked them in. It swept me up in a wave and carried me off to sea.

My life was ruined for what? So she could be with her husband?

The once-firm ground beneath my feet began to shake. The room was spinning. I needed to get an address and end this now.

So I did. After one simple question, she happily shared her address with me. She was hoping for a visit, which only validated and cemented my nausea.

In my mind, this was the phone call that would put her away. Her willingness to share, her joyful recounting of the destruction of my life, provided the keys that would slam her cell door and lock it forever.

I hung up and looked up, trying to draw in one colossal, cleansing breath. Staring right into Detective Blue's eyes, I asked, "Now do you believe me?"

That was a strange question.

In the weeks I had known him, he never insinuated any doubt. But I wasn't asking that question for him.

I was asking for myself.

Part of me had yearned for her to deny everything on the phone call so I could go back to Dr. Michaels and say, "See, I'm not a survivor of childhood sexual abuse after all."

I didn't want to be a survivor of childhood sexual abuse.

I wished I didn't have to be a survivor of childhood sexual abuse.

But the phone call gave me the feeling that I could never run from that again.

Detective Blue put his arm on my shoulder. "Hey, man, I do believe you, and I'm sorry, but we're going to get her."

The second detective stood to leave as well and extended a hand. "Hey, man, you're probably going to hear this a whole lot of times moving forward, but let me be the first to tell you—you're extremely brave."

Brave?

I saw the word float before me, so I shook it off like an annoying fly. I didn't feel brave, and I had never wanted to be brave.

When I walked outside, I gulped in the clean, fresh spring air.

"AAAAAAAHHHHHH!!!!"

I needed a release, and that's all I could think to do. The camp of homeless people who had witnessed me sprint by earlier that day looked up like I was crazy, but that didn't bother me in the least. Over the last few years, I was wise enough to recognize that I was in a dark, lonely place and needed to find the strength and the courage to take some steps out of the pit.

I was brave enough to go to therapy.

I was strong enough to report the abuse.

I was daring enough to meet with a detective.

I was clever enough to make the pretextual phone call happen.

Each step was a step in the right direction.

When the emotion subsided and rational thought took over, I quickly realized my life was about to change drastically. Which meant my wife, parents, and siblings' lives would be changing too.

I owed them all conversations and pulled out my phone to text my parents:

Everything's okay, but we need to talk. It's important. And timely.

My mom's response was exactly what I expected:

I'm in the kitchen. If you'd like to come and find me three
days before Passover, that is where I will be.

I smiled at the predictability of that text, enjoying a small semblance of ordinary after a day that was anything but normal. I began to retrace my steps back past the library and down 500 South to my car. The way back to my car was far less rushed. Instead of sprinting, I strolled. My next phone call was to Sheina.

"Hey, what's up?" Her almost nonchalant response surprised me.

"It worked!"

"*It worked?*" she shouted. "What happened?"

"Get to my parents' house now and I'll tell you everything."

———

True to form, my mom was in the kitchen preparing for Passover. Most of my siblings were home for the holiday at this point, and she was unequivocally clear that this conversation I needed to have could happen in front of everybody.

That wasn't an option.

"Mom, trust me when I tell you, we need to have this conversation in private."

Begrudgingly, she took off her apron and we went to their bedroom.

I was unsure what concerned my parents more: my trepidation or Sheina's look of anticipation.

I took a deep breath and told them everything.

"I just drove here from the Public Safety Building downtown where I participated in a recorded phone call with Vina in which she implicated herself and admitted to numerous acts that qualify as sexual abuse of a child and carry with it a sentence of five years to life."

My father sank onto his bed.

My mother looked at me with a look no child should ever have to see on a parent—horror, shock, confusion. "What?"

"An investigation is now going to proceed. She's here in town, so there is an incentive to move quickly. I don't know if we're talking days or weeks, but this is happening."

The room was still.

Uncomfortable.

"Well," I said when I realized I had to be the one to break the silence. "Do you guys have any questions?"

"No," my father said, bewilderment all over his face. "Welcome home."

Then he patted me on the shoulder and walked out of the room. My mother, however, seemed glued to the ground, her features too painful for me to address.

I showed myself out.

22

Custody

March 28, 2018

Over the next few days, I had a series of difficult conversations.

The first ones were with my siblings. They all deserved to know what had happened, so one by one, I shared everything about what Vina had done and the things I was in the process of doing about it.

My three married siblings were all taken care of by phone. They all responded as best they could, but each conversation carried its own form of confusion, pain, and questions.

The hardest by far were Chaim and Sarahle—the babies of the family, the ones who were raised on Vina's knees. They received their news thanks to a night out with a friend.

"Hey, Avremi! I've got Row 6 seats for the Jazz game tonight. Wanna join us?" texted a friend from the community.

In that moment, the allure of drinking bad beer, yelling loudly at some poor referee just trying to do his job, and casting all my aspirations on ten grown men throwing an orange ball around a 94-foot court seemed like the most welcome distraction known to man.

An hour later, Chaim texted me. My brother heard I was going to the game. He had scored last-minute seats for himself and Sarahle. Could I give them a ride?

If I was going to have to do this in person, the best possible compromise would be not having to make eye contact.

"Guys, I think it's important you know something," I told them during the drive.

I've learned over the years that there is no natural way to bring something like this up. You just have to be honest and authentic.

"Yesterday, the police department recorded a phone call of Vina admitting she sexually abused a young boy several times," I said.

"What?" they said in unison. This wasn't the light pregame conversation they were expecting. "Is that real? How do you know?"

"Well, it's also important you know that I know about this because the child was me."

The car was silent, so I started rambling until we got to the stadium. Then I dropped them off, and that was it.

Discombobulated.

Just like my life.

My next conversation was with Craig. His words of wisdom were the first domino to fall in this whole thing, so I figured it was time to call him and come clean.

"Hey, Craig. Remember when we had lunch in Miami, and I asked you about my friend?"

"The moron?" he shot back, probably sensing my need for a little comedic relief.

"Yeah, that's the one. Listen, I just wanted to let you know I wasn't asking for a member of my community."

"Avremi, I know."

"What? You do?"

"Look, when you're an attorney, everyone asks for a friend. I put two and two together. I'm sorry you went through that, but I'm proud of you for coming forward."

This was a crucial moment for me.

It was one thing to be honest with a therapist or a family member, but Craig? He was a friend, but to a certain extent, he was a stranger. Besides that lunch in Miami and all the vague details I shared, he didn't have any direct affiliation with the story.

The phone call felt freeing.

For years I had wondered what it would be like to share my story with the world; that conversation was my first attempt to dip my toe in the water.

The much harder phone call was the one I had with my mother after we landed in California on Thursday. She was not in a good place. I had gone to say goodbye on my way to the airport, and she hugged me in a way that did not insinuate I was leaving town for nine days. There was a lot unsaid in that hug.

While we were in the air, she had met with Detective Blue and put everything out on the table. She couldn't wrap her mind around how this could've been happening right under her nose and felt tremendous guilt and anger. Detective Blue did his best to explain to her that this is what people like Vina do. My mother didn't miss any signs. This is the game—she is a manipulator.

I did my best to reassure her of everything Detective Blue said. But at some level, it was a helpless feeling. You can't force someone to graduate from one stage and move on to the next, because grief can't be rushed.

My only option was to sit in it with her and listen.

———

Friday was the eve of Passover, one of the busiest days of the year. Although I had many things to do, I called Detective Blue that morning for a quick check-in. It was his day off, and he was only in the office to knock out some paperwork, so he told me there probably wouldn't be much movement.

My to-do list was long enough, so I figured that was probably for the best and tried to put the whole situation out of my mind.

I wasn't expecting much that day.

I certainly wasn't expecting to receive a voicemail that would change everything.

Around 2:30 that afternoon, Immanuel and I headed to Safeway to get some groceries. He's typically very easy to shop with, but for whatever reason, on this day, he was incredibly fussy.

He was cranky.

I was annoyed.

Once we finally managed to get our groceries, we headed back out to the parking lot, and I tried to put him in his car seat, but he wasn't having it. My phone started ringing, but getting to it while also fighting a battle in the back seat with a squirming and crying toddler was hopeless, so I let it go to voicemail.

By the time I got Immanuel fastened in, there was a message in my inbox:

"Avrohom, it's Detective Blue from the Salt Lake City Police Department. Hey, I wanted to let you know we took Vina into custody about two minutes ago. It's about 1545 hours. And ah . . . well anyway . . . if you have any questions or if you just want to talk, give me a call."

Custody?

What?

It worked?

If I just want to talk?

That may have been the best sentence ever uttered between two men discussing such an emotional situation.

Yes, I want to talk!

I immediately called him back, and he explained that he had just shown up at Vina's house with his team and taken her into custody.

"So where is she?" I asked, struggling to wrap my mind around this.

"The Salt Lake County Jail," he said.

"Like the jail part? Not the visitor's part?"

"Avrohom—yes. She's in jail."

I couldn't believe it. I stood in the Safeway parking lot, trying to process everything. Every Powerball has a winner.

———

All hell was breaking loose.

As I spoke to Detective Blue, my mom had gotten up from a quick nap. The voicemail light was flashing on her landline. There was a message from Rodger Florreich, asking my parents if they had any idea where Vina had been taken.

In the few minutes between her being cuffed and escorted to the squad car, and Detective Blue coming back inside to let them know what was happening, Rodger called the only number he thought might help: my parents. I calmed my mother down and finally got back to my in-laws. I dropped off Immanuel with Sheina and feebly attempted to gather some semblance of thought.

Just over seventy-two hours prior, I had thought about sending a pro forma "hey, hope you still remember I exist" email to Detective Blue. The world as I had viewed it that Monday seemed smaller. More wholesome. More peaceful. How many lives had been turned on their heads in the past two and a half days? Was it worth it?

A warm hand on my shoulder pulled me out of my thoughts.

It was my father-in-law. Although Sheina had known about everything for two years, she hadn't told her family until this week, so this was all very fresh for them.

"How do you feel?" he asked. "All better?"

All better?

"No," I said honestly. It felt good to say that. It was the first thing I had been certain of all day. "I don't feel any better."

That was a seminal moment.

My father-in-law's question forced me to come face-to-face with a brutal truth. We may have won this battle, but it didn't fix the gaping wound in my heart. "The system" may be able to provide some semblance of justice, but it's powerless to fix inner wounds.

I did the work. I made the calls. I took as many steps as I could up out of the pit I was in, but I still didn't feel any better.

Her handcuffs didn't equal my healing.

———

As the sun went down in the western sky, I had an eerie suspicion that there may not be enough staircases on this planet to ascend out of the dark pit in my stomach. The darkness felt appropriate. With the onset of the two first days of Passover, I was unplugging and going dark for the next forty-eight hours. A whole 985 miles away, I had set off a bomb and would have to accept the lack of control of not knowing who was wounded by the shrapnel.

I walked inside to a much more cheerful house, and Passover began.

First Seder is a long, drawn-out process that lasts four or five hours, especially with a big family like Sheina's. We drank four glasses of wine, talked about the Exodus, read passages, and sang many songs. My father-in-law is very musically inclined, so it was a beautiful production.

But I sat there stone-faced.

I turned the pages and said the words, but my mind was elsewhere. *Vina's in prison? What do you eat for dinner in prison?*

"Avremi," one of the guests said. "Did you hear what I asked?"

"What? Oh, I'm sorry. Can you repeat the question?"

Where you sit at the long Seder table determines the conversation topics with your neighbors. Sheina had secured us seats in my mother-in-law's corner, and as expected that night, the conversation was all over the place. I thought I was tuning in long enough to follow the thread before retreating into my own head, but I got caught.

"What's your favorite color?" asked a guest trying to find some brevity at 1 a.m.

Favorite color? Really? We're talking about favorite colors?

"Oh right, um, my favorite color is purple."

"Your favorite color is purple?" she said with a snort. "Did something happen to you as a child?"

The table went silent. A few people tried to stifle their laughs. My mother-in-law stared down the guest like she would swallow her alive.

I snorted into my Matzah. "You have no idea."

23

The Hallway

November 15, 2019
1:07 p.m.

I finally ascend the last flight of stairs and push open the door into the fourth-floor hallway. The police officer assigned to the floor gives me a subtle nod as he dutifully keeps watch, scanning the building.

Judge Trease's courtroom is at the very end of the long, narrow west corridor—the last door on the left—W49. To get there, you have to walk past several other courtrooms that may or may not be in session. Sometimes the hallway is empty; other times, it is a zoo.

Today is the former.

The hallway is empty.

It is cooler and brighter than the stairwell, but it allows me the courtesy of being alone with my thoughts for a last few precious seconds.

I've made this walk several times during this long, hellish week of trial.

I've made this walk feeling angry.

I've made this walk feeling resentful.

I've made this walk feeling vindicated.

And now, I have one more opportunity to reflect on everything that happened and try to find some gratitude for each walk.

As I walk down the hallway, I know I can hold my head high. Months earlier, I swore an oath to myself that I would live to see this day. I would outlast my opponent—I would make it.

Deciding to report the abuse was a big win for me, but what I didn't know at the time was Vina's initial arrest was not the end of the story; it was only the beginning. The thought that I'd be able to put this whole thing behind me after Vina was taken into custody was birthed out of blissful ignorance. The arrest was just the start.

The start of all the emails.

The start of all the phone calls.

The start of all the frustration and sleepless nights.

The start of all the games the defense would try to play.

The toughest battles and strongest resistance came after the arrest. The defense played the long game and tried to outlast us. It took every last ounce of my strength and perseverance to overcome. But now, as I walk down the hallway one final time, let the record reflect that I have done it.

The clack of my heels on the marble floor provides a soundtrack for my march toward victory. Like battle drums urging the soldiers on.

My goal was to make it here.

To outlast my opponent.

And here I am.

I am going to walk into that courtroom with my head held high, and no matter what happens, no matter what the jury decides, my head will still be raised at the end. Because regardless of the verdict, I have won.

My definition of victory has nothing to do with jail time. It has everything to do with being heard. And with showing other people that they can be heard too.

I march down the hall as the last several months of politics, games, and learning way more than I expected about the legal system race through my head.

The verdict is in, but regardless of the results, I have done it.

I made it.

I won.

Because I am still standing.

24

Food Fights, Phone Calls, and News Articles

April 1, 2018

When the sun set on Sunday, the first part of Passover ended, and my search for answers began.

Where is she?

What happens next for her?

What happens next for me?

Unfortunately, I quickly learned that answers were going to be difficult to come by. Detective Blue, the one person I knew I could always count on, was now on vacation with his family. With him out of town and out of the loop, no one else was calling me back.

I was losing my mind.

At one point, I even clicked on one of those online ads that promise you can find anyone's criminal history for the low price of $49.95. This probably won't shock you, but when I typed in Vina's name, the super sketchy internet search didn't yield any results.

Then I remembered something. After my original call with Detective

Blue two months prior, I got a phone call from a nice woman who was a victim advocate. She told me to call her if I needed anything. So I did, explaining everything that had happened over the last few days, telling her I'd love to know what was going on with Vina.

"Are you okay?" she asked.

"Yeah, I'm fine," I told her. "I just need some answers."

"Well, I just want to make sure you're okay."

"Look, I don't need emotional support," I shouted. "I need knowledge! This isn't about feelings. I need some facts!"

I hung up on her.

After an entire evening of searching for answers, all I managed to accomplish was hanging up on a friendly victim advocate and donating $50 to some online scam artist.

———

Around 1 p.m. the next afternoon, my phone began hopping off the table. I had set a Google alert on my phone for my name and Vina's.

The arrest hit the press.

Arizona woman arrested on suspicion of 130 counts of sexual abuse of a child, with a picture of her mugshot. The story wasn't just being run in every news outlet in Salt Lake City but by local news affiliates throughout the country.

One hundred thirty was a massive number.

Detective Blue had landed on 130 by combining an estimated seventy episodes that had happened before I turned fourteen, and another sixty after. (Fourteen years old is the line that the law puts in place between abusing a child or a minor.) Drug kingpins who certainly look the part of a criminal mastermind are rarely arrested on 130 counts of anything. The accompanying photo to all of these articles was a mugshot of a grandmotherly figure, sixty-eight years old. Not the sort of criminal anyone was expecting.

Something about seeing the stories and the mug shot felt validating.

It wasn't the pain; I never needed to see Vina hurting. I just wanted the world to acknowledge that someone had hurt me—130 times.

For the next several hours, I read through every single article line by line. As I did, I discovered two really important truths. Neither sat well with me.

The first was that she was out on a $50,000 bail. It turns out the whole "she'll never see the light of day again" thing may have been a little premature.

The second was that she would have an attorney representing her.

Representation? She already admitted it, right? Why does she even have an attorney?

The nice, neat box I was hoping to pack this whole thing into was bursting at the seams.

Meanwhile, the entire world knew about it. People in Tampa Bay were now sitting down with a cup of afternoon tea and reading my story.

Florida? Really?

The story was spreading fast, and the further it went, the more anxious I became about my anonymity. Sure, police reports aren't a matter of public record, great. However, this was quickly becoming something much larger.

At the time, as a matter of principle, I was absolutely convinced I would never become "the guy who was sexually abused." In my insular religious community, I knew that would become the central theme of my life forever.

It would be my brand. I could cure cancer, but in my community, I would still be the guy who was sexually abused.

There was no way I would be doing that.

I needed my name to remain out of this story at all costs.

———

After putting the boys to bed that evening, I sat down to relax when another Google alert pinged. My story was the top story on the 9 o'clock news.

I clicked on the link and was taken to the ABC4 newscast. Nick McGurk was telling my story. But he wasn't just rehashing the already widely spread details. He and his cameraman had gone downtown to get a comment from the district attorney.

The screen cut away, and there sat D.A. Sim Gill holding a folder in his hand, talking about my case. There's a good chance that the folder was just a visual prop, but part of me allowed the idea that he was actually holding the reports from my interview.

"We encourage victims to come forward, no matter how much time has elapsed," he explained. "These are cases we take seriously as an office. We'll make sure justice is served."

These cases.

My case.

Being taken seriously.

Leading off the 9 o'clock news.

I choked back a sob. It was a reassurance I hadn't known I wanted but so desperately needed. The system may be long-winded and slow, but somewhere out there, my case was being taken seriously.

———

Despite the case picking up momentum and drama, I still had a life to lead and a family to take care of. Sheina and I were in the market for a new home. Menachem had come around in the summer of 2017, and we were looking for a slightly bigger house. Finding a new home in our community can be tricky. We needed it to be within walking distance of the synagogue, so the net we could cast was only so big, and houses rarely came on the market around us.

On Tuesday morning, I got a call from our realtor. "There's a house that came on the market. It's two stories and in your price range. Do you want me to put in an offer?"

Why not? We're just 985 miles away, going through a life-altering event.

"Sure," I said after Sheina and I looked at a few pictures. "Put in an offer."

———

On Wednesday, we took the kids on a trip with all their cousins to Happy Hollow. The kids were getting restless in the back seat, and as every parent knows, there are only so many ways to keep them amused. Out of options, they had resorted to throwing their snacks at each other. Immanuel's aim was immeasurably better than his nine-month-old brother.

In the middle of all that, my phone rang. A 385 number I didn't recognize.

Gulp. A part of me sensed this was it.

"Hi, is this Mr. Zippel?"

"It is."

"Hello, my name is Amy Kershisnik, and I am a social worker for the Salt Lake County District Attorney's office. I'm sitting here with Senior Deputy District Attorney Donna Kelly. Do you have a few minutes to talk?"

"Of course," I said. "But there is currently a food fight going on in my back seat. Can I get my kids dropped off with my wife and then call you right back?"

When I did, Donna explained that she would be the prosecutor on my case moving forward. "We screened the case this morning and our office has decided to charge the defendant with five counts of aggravated sexual abuse of a child, which are first-degree felonies, and two counts of forcible sexual abuse, which are second-degree felonies."

You what now? Did she just say screened?

In my mind's eye, screens were either for windows or Rudy Gobert during a pick-and-roll.

More importantly, did she just say two and five?

The whole world exploded before me as I counted in my head.

Let's see, one, two, three, four, five plus two is seven.

"Okay," I said, trying to keep my cool.

"We understand that you are currently out of state, but we'd love to sit down and meet with you when you get back."

"Right. Hey, can I ask you something?"

"Sure."

"Yeah, what happened to the other 123 counts?"

"That's a complicated question," she responded calmly. "But I'd be happy to explain that to you in person. Is that okay with you?"

"I guess so," I said, feeling like I just got completely screwed by the system.

"One more thing," she said before hanging up. "I know your anonymity is very important to you. Our office has released a charging document called an 'information,' where you will only be identified by your initials, not your name. But do know that once they file the charges, there will be a formal press release, so you can expect another round of articles."

When I hung up with Donna, I immediately called Dr. Michaels, and he gave me a rare piece of advice. He knew how hungry I'd be for information throughout the process and suggested I hire a private attorney, someone who worked for me, not the state. Later that afternoon, I hired Annie Taliaferro, a defense attorney by trade who had worked with victims like me in the past.

Things were happening fast. In one day, my team grew substantially. It now consisted of Donna and Amy from the D.A.'s office and Annie, my own personal attorney.

I started to feel like I was getting ready for war.

———

That evening I had to drive to Oakland to return a rental car, and my phone started blowing up again. That was a familiar feeling by now. I knew what was happening—the second press release. I quickly pulled over to the side of the highway and started reading.

This round had a little more meat and potatoes.

It talked about how Vina was formally charged with seven felonies. All of it was pretty standard until I read a line that I was definitely not expecting: "There were multiple incidents in the victim's youth, many of which involved the perpetrator touching the young boy's penis."

Five little letters jumped off the screen and smacked me across the face.

Really?

It was one thing to say "sexually abused" and let people's minds take that where they would. But no, the article decided to leave nothing up to the imagination, sparing no detail besides my name.

There I was, sitting on the side of the highway in Northern California by myself, reeling while reading a public news story about my privates.

I swore once again, on all that was good and holy, that I would never ever let anyone know it was me.

Before I could even pull back on the highway, my phone rang again. This time it wasn't a Google alert about a news article talking publicly about a very private matter.

It was my realtor. "Hey, Avremi, the offer went through. Congratulations, you just bought a house."

Of course. That may as well happen.

It was the least amount of thought I've ever given to a massive life decision. When I got home that night, I was eager to share with Sheina everything that was happening.

"Well, I've got big news and weird news," I told her. "We just bought a house I'm not sure we want, and my genitals are in the news."

———

On Monday, we were finally back in Salt Lake City, and I drove to the District Attorney's office to meet with Donna.

If you are a citizen entering the D.A.'s office, you are likely in the middle of one of the worst days of your life, and the environment does not help.

It's bleak.

The secretary sits behind bulletproof glass.

The sheriff's deputy stands next to the metal detector, weapon in hand.

It's a cold, sterile environment that needs to be protected by law enforcement.

Definitely not the place where you want to spill your guts.

I walked in and told them who I was, and a few minutes later, Amy came out to get me and bring me back to her office. We sat around and talked for a few minutes, and then Donna walked in. I'll never forget that moment. The folders they use in the D.A.'s office are huge. Donna walked in holding my folder with the words "Special Victims Unit."

My whole life came full circle.

Years ago, I laid in bed watching *SVU* . . .

Now I'm in the show.

As soon as Donna sat down, we had it out.

"What happened to the other 123?" I asked, coming out swinging.

"A crime has elements," she explained calmly. "My job is to prove every criminal element beyond a reasonable doubt." When she sat down and listened to my recorded phone call with Vina, she was able to identify seven counts.

Screenings had once belonged in theaters, and elements were once parts of science experiments. I yearned for a simpler life.

One hundred thirty had been an estimate.

We were going with seven.

It took a while, but she eventually convinced me that was the right move. She made the compelling argument that I had an emotional attachment to 130. That stung for a bit, but she was right. One hundred thirty had become my companion, my validation. I leaned on that number for a week, but now I had to say goodbye.

So I did.

One hundred thirty was history.

The operative number was now seven.

"Don't get stressed out about the numbers," she said in closing. "We have five first-degree felonies to focus on, which is more than enough. Each one of those first-degree felonies carries with it five to life."

By the time she assured me most cases have one to two first-degree felonies and that five was almost unheard of, I was satisfied.

But that peace didn't last long because her next bit of news wasn't what I wanted to hear.

"Remember, Avremi, this will be a long journey."

"How long are we talking?" I asked, not sure that I wanted to hear the answer.

"Are you aware that the initial appearance is May 9?"

"I am."

"Well, just get used to there typically being sixty to ninety days between every hearing from there on out."

Sixty to ninety days between hearings?

According to what I'd learned from NBC, the gap between crime and sentence is five days max.

This was not what I was expecting. Indeed, we were embarking on a long journey together—a journey to justice. A journey that would feel different every day of my life.

Together, we'd figure out what that meant.

25

The Initial Appearance

May 9, 2018

Everyone told me not to go, but I wanted to be there.

The initial appearance never makes the forty-four-minute episode of SVU. There's nothing glamorous or glorifying about it. Instead, the defendant stands up before a judge and is asked a basic statement: "Do you understand the nature of the charges against you?"

Their response is either *yes* or *no*.

That's it.

Nobody understood why I was so determined to go, and truthfully, I didn't even know myself. I just knew I needed to be there.

As I would come to find out, it had nothing to do with the question being asked to the defendant and everything to do with a more profound question I was asking myself. A deeper battle was being fought below the surface, and I went to the initial appearance to win it.

When I showed up at the courthouse, I quickly learned what a motion calendar is. When judges have shorter, five- to ten-minute hearings, they call motion hearings.

In the interest of efficiency, judges will schedule thirty to sixty

motion hearings in a single morning. This means thirty-sixty defen-
dants and their victims are told their hearing is on Monday at 8:30, and
everyone shows up to the courtroom, heads to the fourth floor where
the motion hearings are held, and waits for their five minutes of fame.

I woke up that morning to go to court.

A serious place.

Official business.

I walked in expecting a somber, quiet, professional atmosphere.

Instead, it was like a chicken market.

There were dozens of people coming and going. Some attorneys
were introducing themselves to their clients, and other attorneys were
running around trying to identify who their clients even were.

I felt like we were all standing at a crowded gate in the airport, waiting to hear if our flight was departing or not.

Court is sacred in our minds—but it can be a jungle in reality.

After weaving in and out of the crowd for a few minutes, I gave up
searching for answers and headed to the fourth-floor lobby.

The front of the Matheson Courthouse is made entirely of glass.
When you stand in the lobby of the fourth floor, you can look out at
a great view of the city. You see cars zooming by on their way to work,
pedestrians strolling by on their morning walk, and other ordinary,
everyday people who aren't caught up in a court case living normal lives.

It's a great place to people watch.

I stood there for a few minutes, letting my mind wander, hoping all
the people who passed by were doing something more inspiring with
their days than attending an initial appearance.

Then Vina pulled up, and the world stopped.

This was my first time seeing her since everything happened.

From my fourth-floor vantage point, I watched her climb out of the
car with Rodger. I was expecting to see her defeated, distraught, down-
trodden, and apologetic. Instead, she strolled up with a smile on her face.

Their son was waiting for them at the entrance, and they walked right up to him and gave him a huge hug, embracing him with joy.

Wait a minute, what?

They were hugging.

They were laughing.

They seemed to sense excitement in the air.

And I was perplexed.

Is she here for her court date or a family reunion? Aren't we talking about a serious crime? Shouldn't she be scared? Or at the very least concerned? Is she not getting it?

That was the moment I realized why I wanted to be there so badly. I knew why I needed to see her. It wasn't just to watch her from a safe vantage point on the fourth floor; I needed to look her in the eyes. I needed to make eye contact with her and let her know that this was real and that I meant business.

This wasn't a joke.

I was serious.

It occurred to me that I never used to look her in the eyes. For years, I was so ashamed. I knew she knew everything. So every time we made eye contact, I would immediately look down. I'd break first.

She'd had the upper hand over me since I was eight years old.

All of that was about to change.

Right before she entered the courtroom, we locked eyes. I was sitting on the other side of the hallway, and her stare met mine. This time, I didn't look away. I looked straight into her eyes with the conviction of someone who understood the tables had turned.

I held it.

She dropped it.

I was looking at her.

She was looking at the ground.

For the first time in my life, I realized my perception of myself mattered to me more than her perception of me. And that is why I showed up for the initial appearance.

On paper, everyone was right. The initial appearance was a waste of time. It was chaotic, confusing, and time-consuming. Even though it took all morning, the actual event—Vina standing before a judge—lasted all of thirty seconds. The judge didn't even read the charges. He just let us all know July 17 would be our prelim.

To the rest of the world, the whole day was insignificant. I could've stayed home; an email would've sufficed.

But for me, it was infinitely significant.

I would've sat through a thousand initial appearances for that moment. The moment I realized my abuser no longer had the upper hand in my life. She no longer had the power. The tables had turned.

I knew it as soon as she looked away.

26

Long-Term Stayed

July 16, 2018

July 17 was shaping up to be a big day.

That was the date of the preliminary hearing where I would be called up on the stand in front of a real judge to testify. It's not a trial, but it's meant to be a preview of it, where the prosecution has to present some evidence to convince a judge that they have a credible case.

At this point, I'd made it clear to Donna a hundred times that I wanted to remain anonymous. She went to great lengths to try to honor that request. However, she was always very honest and explained that this was an open hearing.

She would have to use my full name.

No more initials.

In an open court with real people and potentially real press.

There was no law stopping any journalist from walking out of that courtroom and announcing to the world the victim's name is Avremi Zippel. Every journalist I've ever worked with has standards; each of them would've respected my request. However, they didn't have to. There was no law stopping them, so Donna couldn't make any promises.

Guarantees were off the table.

I was nervous.

On the day before the hearing, I got an email informing me that we had a much bigger problem on our hands.

The email was from Annie:

> **Donna just called. The defense attorneys have filed a petition for competency. The hearing will be stayed. It won't happen tomorrow. Let's still go to court at 9 a.m. tomorrow, and we'll talk to Donna and go from there. Just know there won't be a hearing, so you can call off your family and anyone who may want to attend.**

Stayed? What the hell does that mean? That's not even proper grammar. And what's a petition for competency?

I knew that in the criminal defense system, there was something called "not guilty by reason of insanity." If you prove that you are clinically insane, you'll go to a state hospital instead of prison.

This was not that.

Annie explained that under the United States Constitution, a defendant is guaranteed a right to assist in their own defense. If a defendant is incompetent, it means they are unable to assist in that defense. It means the person is so out of it that they can't even differentiate between the judge, jury, and attorneys.

The defense counsel wasn't trying to argue Vina was crazy during the decade of abuse. They were trying to prove she was currently incompetent.

That was their move.

They were filing a motion asking the court to evaluate her for incompetency.

You've got to be freaking kidding me.

We were talking about the person I had just had a forty-minute conversation with on the phone. The one who recalled events from fifteen years ago in graphic, vivid, and sickening detail. She sounded pretty competent to me.

Adding to the frustration was my newly acquired knowledge about how the system works in the real world. "Today we'll figure out a good time to have a hearing thirty days from now. At that hearing, we'll determine who the evaluator will be so that thirty days from then, they can evaluate her."

This was going to take forever.

For something that is plain as day.

Just listen to the phone call!

———

I was furious.

Sitting in the courtroom the next day just made it worse. The hearing was an unmitigated disaster, and that's putting it nicely. Vina's defense counsel stumbled through the motion, and the judge didn't seem to even know how the whole process was supposed to work.

That was the darkest moment of the entire journey for me.

As I sat in my seat, watching the whole thing unravel before my eyes, I had one thing on my mind:

Everyone had lied to me.

They told me to go to therapy and things would get better.

They told me to call the police and things would get better.

They told me to press charges and things would get better.

I did everything I was supposed to do. I ran every play I was supposed to run. I followed the playbook to a T, and where did it get me?

Lying flat on my back like Charlie Brown trying to kick a football. Because at the end of the day, the people who do these sorts of things get away with it.

It's as fictional as an *SVU* episode—based on truths but full of fantasy.

You end up right back where you started.

Revictimized.

Retraumatized.

On your back, watching Lucy laugh at you while she walks away, football in hand.

My team and I went into one of the private closets beside the courtroom, and there was smoke coming out of my ears.

"This is going to take some time," Donna started, ever the straight shooter. "We aren't going to rush this. I refuse to settle for an unfair evaluator and risk anything."

I couldn't believe it. The whole thing was unraveling right before my eyes. "Could this work for them?" That's what I needed to know. "Could their strategy work? Could they actually get away with this?"

Donna looked down, which is never a good sign, but then to her credit raised her head back up and locked eyes with me.

"I'd be lying if I said no. The evaluators are professionals, but if they find her incompetent, it'll get pushed back. They'll reevaluate her once a year, but she'll be at home in between. For all intents and purposes, this would go away. She'd be free a year at a time."

The ground was shifting beneath my feet.

"Look," Annie chimed in. "I've tried to pull this move before. I'll bet you a steak dinner it won't work. It'll be okay; she'll come back competent."

"There's no Kosher steak in Utah anyway," I said, lashing out at her. Then I decided the meeting was over and stormed out, looking for something to break, burn, or yell at.

———

I brought that anger home, and my wife and kids had to deal with a very absent-minded and on-edge version of me that I'm not proud of.

I was livid.

I was emotional.

I wanted revenge.

Above all else, I needed to control something.

I know what I'll do; I'll file a civil suit. Fight fire with fire.

I knew you couldn't plead incompetence to a civil suit, so I decided to take matters into my own hands and sue her. I needed an attorney (not to mention a good amount of money) to do that. I picked up my phone and called Annie, not even exchanging pleasantries before explaining my master plan to her.

"Okay, Avremi. I hear you," she said calmly. "That's certainly something you could do, and I would be more than happy to be your attorney."

"Great! I'll get in my car right now, and we'll . . ."

"Avremi," she said, cutting me off. "I will tell you what. I'm heading out of town for the week. This is a big decision. Let's take a couple days to think about it and connect when I get back."

That wasn't the answer I wanted . . . but it was the answer I needed.

Looking back, I know what Annie was doing, and I'm thankful for it. She knew cooler heads would prevail and was giving me some time to cool off before I made an irrational decision.

However, at the time, I didn't like that answer. I agreed begrudgingly and spent the next twenty-four hours moping around the house, wallowing in my misery.

I was angry.

I was sad.

I was hurt.

I spent the whole next day looking for things to do, looking for something to numb the pain. As luck would have it, the ESPY Awards were on that night. The ESPYs are an award show ESPN puts on every summer to celebrate and remember the best moments in sports that year. It's the Oscars of sports.

The best play of the year is always the most exciting to watch.

The best game of the year always brings up nostalgia.

But the most moving part of the night usually belongs to the Arthur Ashe Courage Award. It's a moment to honor an athlete who displayed courage in the face of adversity.

In 2018, however, it wasn't given to a single athlete. It was given to dozens and dozens of athletes—the "sister survivors" who had been sexually abused for decades by Larry Nassar.

As the music started, the entire crowd stood to their feet to honor and applaud the courage of 141 survivors who were flooding the stage from every angle. Reading a number like 141 is one thing, but it hits differently when you see them all walking together. They just kept on coming from every side of the room, the sheer magnitude of the situation hitting me like a ton of bricks.

Each one is not just a number; they are a human being.

There are no words to describe the segment; it was incredible. Not one person in the theater sat for the entire ten minutes.

I laid on my couch and cried like a baby, unable to contain my emotions.

On one level, it was the worst possible thing for me to watch.

On another, it was exactly what I needed.

Sarah Klein, Tiffany Lopez, and Aly Raisman stood in the front as the spokeswomen. As Sarah started, a truth hit me and began to settle in my soul—a truth that was brutally difficult for me to comprehend but would be unequivocally important for the road ahead.

This was 2018. I knew enough about the Nassar case to know that Sarah was believed to be Nassar's first victim. He had abused her back in 1988. Meaning, as amazing as this moment was, it didn't atone for the heavy reality that it was also almost thirty years in the making. It took nearly three decades to get to this point.

That's what the defense counsel does. When they know they are clearly in the wrong, their only play is to try to run out the clock. Bog it down with motions. Add six months here and another twelve months there, and see if you can outlast your opponent.

As I laid in my living room, the fire erupted deep inside me again—this time not as a spark but as a blazing wildfire. I swore to myself that, come hell or high water—whatever blood, sweat, tears, or guts it took out of me—I would persevere.

Competency nonsense? Evaluators?

Sure. What else do you got?

Throw it at me.

Throw as many obstacles as you want at me until kingdom come.

Because if this is a patience game, I will outlast you.

I knew the journey would be longer and lonelier than I had hoped, but that didn't matter because I was in it for the long haul. Patience, as it turns out, is the opposite of control. But if patience was a prerequisite for justice, I would learn it.

Aly ended the segment with one of her classic mic drops.

"We can draw strength from each other," she reminded us. "We may suffer alone, but we survive together."

The Facebook message Vina sent to the boy in our community flashed through my mind. This wasn't just about me. This was about us surviving together. Winning this battle was the small part I could play in the war.

I will outlive you.

I will outlast you.

I will outwait you.

You manipulated me once.

You aren't going to do it again.

27

The Courtroom

November 15, 2019
1:09 p.m.

Judge Trease's courtroom is all the way at the end of the hallway.

When I reach the end, I take a left, open the double doors, and take my first step into the courtroom where I've spent the last four days of hell.

The courtroom feels different.

There is a different kind of tension in the air.

All week was stressful, but now it's at a new level. You can cut the tension with a knife.

I walk up and take my usual seat in the single chair beside the first bench on the prosecution's side. This time, however, I pass a new addition to the courtroom: two armed deputies standing between our table and Vina's table, neither looking particularly cheerful.

I sit down and take a deep breath as, one by one, Team Avremi find their seats. Each of them has rallied around me during the months of preparation and then battled alongside me for all four days of court.

All of us have done it to get to this moment.

The verdict.

Annie isn't going to be able to make it back, so Amy slides into the spot right beside me as Donna takes her well-worn seat in front of us. Sheina and my mother sit down to Amy's right. To my delight and my mother's relief, my father enters and takes his seat directly behind me. Somehow he has managed to make it back in time. There are times in life when you break whatever traffic laws you need to break to be somewhere—this is one of those moments for him.

The seating arrangement is fitting; it reminds me that although I have felt like I was fighting much of this battle alone, I have always had a team I loved fighting alongside me and watching my back.

We are seconds away from the moment.

The verdict is about to be read.

I take one last glance ahead of me and see Detective Blue sitting in his chair, his face calm but focused. He is well-trained and ready to handle these types of moments, whatever the outcome.

Just before the doors close, one last person slips in and takes her post—Gillian Friedman. I'm glad she's here. Gillian has played a massive role in getting us to this point. With everything that has happened, it wouldn't feel right to hear the verdict without her.

I give her a quick smile and a subtle wink. She returns it.

"All rise!" calls out the deputy at the door to the judge's chambers. "Third District Court now in session. The Honorable Vernice S. Trease presiding."

28

Tell My Story?

Late 2018

Sheina and I chose a unique life path.

We are one of the 5,000 couples around the globe that represent the Chabad movement. It's the world's largest Jewish outreach movement, and we help run the Salt Lake City branch alongside my parents.

Instead of sitting around waiting for Jews to come to us, we try to take our message to the streets. We do our best to share and show the beauty of our heritage and its lifestyle with Jews who would otherwise not be interested in having much of a connection with it—Judaism Salesmanship 101.

As we started developing our work in 2017, one of the first big things we did was throw a Purim party to connect with young adults. Purim is one of the most joyous days on the Jewish calendar; we throw parties to commemorate a woman named Esther who found the courage to approach the king of Persia and save her people.

One of the young ladies who came to the party was named Gillian Friedman. She had just moved to town from Seattle to work at Goldman Sachs, and she showed up wanting to get involved in the community. She must've enjoyed herself too because she agreed to come to our house for Shabbat dinner a few weeks later.

Then she fell off the face of the earth, which people tend to do. It's part and parcel of directing a community of young adults in the flakiest generation in the history of humanity. At that point, Sheina and I were well-accustomed to getting ghosted.

———

"A Rabbi walks into a bar . . ."

Every time I enter Wasatch Brewery, I feel like it's a setup for a bad joke. But that's not why I was going. I walked into the pub in July of 2018 to get drinks with a new member of the community who had just moved to Salt Lake City.

When I walked out onto the patio, I looked over in the back corner and there was a man with his back turned to me wearing a kippah—a dead giveaway. When I made my way over to him, I noticed a woman was sitting at the table with him.

That was not what I expected.

Well, this is awkward. I didn't know I was supposed to bring a plus-one—I should've invited Sheina.

Then I got closer to the table and realized he wasn't sitting with his wife; instead, it was none other than Gillian Friedman. She happened to be there with other friends and just stopped by to say hello.

"Hey, Gillian!" I said, sitting down at the table and taking a few minutes to catch up. "How are things at Goldman Sachs?"

"I'm actually not there anymore," she said. "I got a job at the *Deseret News*. I'm an investigative reporter."

Investigative reporter?

Those two words had the same effect on me as Craig's words had six months earlier when he told me he was a former prosecutor. A prosecutor was what I needed back then, and there was a good and growing chance that an investigative reporter would be what I would need in the near future.

"Really?" I said. "Good for you."

And good for me to know.

We talked for a few more minutes and then said goodbye. Gillian headed out, and this fellow and I got into our conversation as I filed that potentially useful bit of information into the back of my mind.

I now know an investigative reporter.

Another arrow in my quiver.

———

Donna was checking in with me regularly, but there wasn't much to report. The case was crawling along at a snail's pace.

After the original July 17 prelim got canceled, the search for an evaluator began.

The next meaningful event was a court date in early September, sixty days after the canceled prelim. I showed up at the courthouse, went through security, and sat down, all to hear the judge schedule another hearing in sixty days.

"Any movement on this case?" Judge Trease asked.

"No, Your Honor."

"Okay then, let's do this again in November."

Our system at work.

Going to that hearing was probably not good for my mental health, but I refused to miss it. I refused to miss any of them. I went to each one to send a message: You will not run out the clock on me. You will see my face at every hearing, even if my attendance is a futile waste of time, to remind myself and to remind you that you will not burn out my desire for justice.

———

On October 26, I got an email from Donna out of the blue.

Good news, the defendant has been found competent

by the evaluator. The next appearance date is November 19 at 8:30. I will ask the judge to find the defendant competent to proceed. Defense can object and ask for a hearing; we shall see what they do.

An email had never made me so emotional before, but a few tears began to stream down my face as I sat at my desk, reading her words. It took three months, but we won. It may have been a small win, but it was a win.

But it was far from over.

In this situation, the defense reserves the option to challenge the competency hearing, and they had insinuated to Donna that they would do so. They could object and ask for a hearing before the judge so the judge could decide.

Which, of course, would push things back another few months.

Again.

———

Over the summer, Detective Blue and I had reconnected by email. He had heard about the incompetence motion and wanted to offer his support. He shared with me that he had been sidelined by some needed surgeries after hopping too many fences chasing bad guys. I updated him on our ever-so-slight progress, and he responded back, asking for details about the November 19 hearing.

We were still a long way off from the actual trial where we'd ask him to testify. He'd be subpoenaed for trial, but there was no reason for him to come to this hearing. It was a single hearing in a case he had been involved with six months prior. There are hundreds of those types of hearings for a guy like him. Often, cops don't even show up to hearings they are subpoenaed for.

But when I walked into the courthouse on November 19, he was standing there waiting for me.

I gave him a big hug.

It was the first time I'd seen Detective Blue in person since the pretextual phone call eight months earlier. A reminder of simpler times. Back when it was just him and me and that was it. Now there were attorneys, judges, motions, and hearings—everything had changed. Having him by my side infused me with the confidence I needed to face the hearing.

By this point, I had learned to mentally prepare myself for the worst-case scenario. I was ready for the defense counsel to get up and challenge the evaluation and push this thing back another few months.

But that didn't happen.

The defense counsel stood up and said, "Your Honor, at this time, we do not challenge the finding of the evaluation."

Whoa.

That's not what I expected.

This began a pattern. The defense counsel talked a really big game until they showed up in court and ran away from it—like a bluff.

Detective Blue slapped me on the knee.

Victory!

It may have been a small victory, but a win is a win. We got an out. We may have to get twenty-seven outs to win the game, but we were heading in the right direction.

Vina was found competent.

So what did that mean? The prelim was stayed or indefinitely postponed while we figured out the defendant's competency. Now that we'd figured that out, we had to "unstay" the prelim.

"Okay, counsel," Judge Trease said. "Let's put a prelim on the calendar."

"Your Honor," the defense counsel said, pulling out an old-school agenda. "I'm just looking through my calendar. I've got trial after trial coming up. It'll have to be in the new year."

This was the first time I saw the defense counsel pull that tactic. Unfortunately, it would become a pattern, a strategy to attempt to prolong the inevitable.

Donna had a philosophy. She was never going to rush the defense counsel. If you do, they'd appeal the case and cry, "The counsel was rushed into trial and didn't have sufficient time."

I didn't like that philosophy one bit, but I knew it was the right move. "Okay," Judge Trease said. "We're going to have a preliminary hearing on February 5."

Unbelievable.

That's how this is going to go.

But you know what, do your worst.

I can wait.

February? March? Two years from now?

You aren't going to outwait me.

———

Confidentiality was starting to feel like a roll of the dice. There was a good chance my name would remain off the table, but playing the odds was beginning to feel irresponsible with something this important.

The problem was, if I took my chances and someone did decide to leak my name, I would have no control of the story. It could be someone who really didn't know me or my story rolling all the gritty details out to the world. And the only thing that would be more nauseating than my story going public was to have the wrong version of my story going public.

I did have another option.

I could come out and tell my story on my own.

The way I wanted to say it.

At the time I wanted to tell it.

And by now, I had told quite a few people, and every time I did, I was met with either sorrow or solidarity—but never judgment. It hadn't been nearly as bad as I thought. Of course, I was telling people I deemed safe. Going public would mean opening myself up to all the internet trolls in the world, people who say terrible things behind the safety of a screen just to cause pain in the world.

That thought wasn't scaring me nearly as bad as it used to. It was starting to feel like something I could handle. I was beginning to understand a larger reality. My concern about the way the world perceived the story was actually rooted in the way I perceived the story. If I thought the world would react with ridicule, mockery, and disdain, that's because I wasn't in a good place with myself at that moment. On the other hand, if I found that the world was reacting to me with empathy, kindness, and grace, well, guess what? That's because I was reacting to myself with empathy, kindness, and grace.

Apparently, therapy was doing something.

Plus, I had a way to do it—Gillian Friedman of the *Deseret News*. So I pulled out my phone, took a deep breath, and made a risky phone call.

"Do me a favor," I said to Gillian on the other line. "Go on your computer and Google Alavina Florreich."

"My God," she said a few seconds later. "Looks like she was arrested on 130 counts of sexual abuse of a child."

I held a very dramatic pause. I still had a hard time connecting myself to the story and wished she would've arrived at the point on her own, but it didn't happen.

"That child was me."

I'd known Gillian to be someone who's very passionate; however, at that moment, she maintained total professionalism. "Wow, okay, thank you for sharing."

"I'm coming to you because I need some advice. I still don't know if I'm ready to tell the world. You know our community—you know how big of a risk this would be. But I'm wondering what it would look like to tell my story on my terms."

"You know what," she said calmly. "Let's go get some coffee. Rose Establishment?"

The Rose Establishment is one of those trendy, overpriced coffee shops downtown that investigative reporters like to hang out in.

"Sounds good."

———

We sat down, and I started telling Gillian my story. I told her about the scheduled prelim, the anonymity I'd been granted so far, and the fear I had about getting out in front of this story.

"Here's the deal," I told her, finally getting to my point. "I need to find a journalist I can trust."

Gillian dug into that statement quite a bit.

"Well, Avremi, if I agree to tell your story, it's crucial you understand one thing. I am not your ghostwriter. I don't work for you. I'll interview you, and you can decide to tell me or not tell me whatever you want, but at the end of the day, I'd be telling your story on behalf of the *Deseret News*."

I could sense where this was heading before she said it.

"Meaning, you will not have editorial oversight," she continued. "Once I write it, I will fact-check it with you, but you will not have the ability to decide what does and does not go in."

"Okay, cool," I said. "This was a fact-finding mission, and you've helped me find facts. Thanks for meeting with me."

———

Around that time, I went to a community event and met United States Congressman Chris Stewart, the man who co-wrote Elizabeth Smart's book, *My Story*.

Elizabeth was kidnapped when she was young and went through nine months of hell before finally being rescued. I grew up a few minutes down the street from Elizabeth and remember the event vividly—the lost posters, the efforts of the search-and-rescue teams, the fear, and the anger. I also remember the joy and celebration when she was found. More than anything, I remember her courage and the way she publicly and courageously shared her story. By sharing her story, she's helped millions of people through the most difficult moments of their lives.

"Congressman, can I speak to you privately for a moment?"

"Of course," Chris said and led me to a back room.

"I just wanted to let you know I think the job you did on Elizabeth's book was incredible. Beyond meaning that as a general compliment, the book meant a lot to me."

"Why's that?" he asked curiously.

At that point, I still couldn't bring myself to say the words "I'm a survivor of childhood sexual abuse." So instead, I said, "I don't know if you heard, but back in April, a woman was arrested here in town for 130 cases of childhood sexual abuse. That child was me."

"Wow," he said, visibly taken aback. "Well, Rabbi, thank you for sharing. I'm encouraged by your bravery."

I thanked him and began to walk away.

"Hey, Avremi," he said. "Would you find it beneficial to connect with Elizabeth?"

"What? I mean, yeah. Of course. But why would Elizabeth want to connect with me?"

"Well, I think you'll be surprised. She's the kind of person who will make time for someone when she knows they'll benefit from it. I'm going to put you in touch."

Sure you will.

———

On January 8, 2019, I walked out of a meeting and had a voicemail.

"Hi, this is Elizabeth Smart. Chris Stewart is a mutual friend of ours, and he suggested that I should give you a phone call because you are dealing with something. Anyway, feel free to call me if you want to chat."

Wait . . . Elizabeth Smart has my phone number?

I'm not going to lie—I was a little starstruck. I called her back and only had one single question for her.

I vividly remember sitting around tables, hearing adults snicker at the conspiracy theory that she was gone for nine months because her parents wanted her to get pregnant at an early age.

Which is an awful thing to say.

A blatant lie.

But people talk.

That was my one question for Elizabeth. "How do you rise above the noise? How do you refuse to get bogged down by the trolls? Does it ever bother you?"

"I hear the noise," she said after listening intently. "Although I try not to read the comments, from time to time, I do. The thing is, my story helps others, and what I gain from giving value to other people makes it all worth it—trolls and all."

Just a few months earlier, I was sitting on the side of the highway, reading an article with my initials in it talking about my sexual abuse, swearing I would never let the world know the name behind the initials.

The trolls were going to have a heyday.

Their derision terrified me.

And now, here I was a few months later, on the phone with Elizabeth Smart, a person who knows more about the trolls than almost anyone, listening to her assure me it's worth it.

"Would you like to meet up and chat in person?" she asked, probably sensing my internal conflict.

"That would be great."

———

Meanwhile, Gillian was looking into my story, investigating whether or not she could tell it.

There were layers and layers of approval she needed to get to even consider moving forward, but in January of 2019, she called to let me know she was in if I was.

Her *maybe* had turned into a *yes*.

She was wondering if the same was true for me.

A conversation that week with a respected Rabbi in our community would help me make my decision.

"Rabbi, from a philosophical standpoint, is going public the right thing to do?"

"I'm not going to tell you what to do," he said. "If you go public, it will probably help a lot of people. But I don't know what will happen to your kids' marriage prospects."

"Rabbi, my kids are one and three. They will get married twenty years from now."

"I know," he said. "And I repeat what I said. I don't know what will happen to their marriage prospects. We know how rampant this issue is in our community, and we know speaking about it more will help. What we don't know is what will happen to the first person who speaks out."

So now I had two issues: faceless trolls who make comments about me getting lucky at fourteen, and a community that is so uncomfortable with this topic that it may affect my kids' marriage prospects in two decades.

My insecurities about being a bad dad have always been in the back of my mind. Going public wasn't just going to affect me; it could cause generations of pain for my family.

———

The next day I drove up to Park City to have coffee with Elizabeth, unsure what possessed me to do such a thing.

What am I going to say to her?

She was kind enough to give me a few minutes on the phone, but did I really need to pull her away from her busy life?

I'll never forget the moment she walked into the coffee shop, car seat in hand. I saw her face, the exact same face I vividly remember seeing plastered on every street corner.

Here she is now, walking into Starbucks on a cold January morning, carrying her baby in a car seat.

That moment is etched into my memory.

It was the moment I realized no one cares how much you know until they know how much you care. If you want to make an impact on someone's life, show up to coffee in the middle of a snowstorm, baby in hand.

That's advocacy.

Advocacy is not the speech. It's not the tweet. It's not the photoshoot.

Advocacy is pausing your busy life to drive through the snow and sit down for coffee with someone who needs a friend.

As we sat down for coffee—well, I had coffee, she had seltzer water—I told her about Gillian and the opportunity I had to tell my story.

I think I was expecting her to tell me what to do, but she didn't. That's not what she does. Elizabeth never attempts to have all the answers. Instead, she just shares her experiences. She doesn't promise people it's all going to be okay. Instead, she just assures people that she's been through similar struggles and lets them know she is pulling for them and is with them.

Solidarity.

That's it.

That's all it took.

I walked out of that Starbucks feeling like I had superpowers. Like I could forego my car and fly back to Salt Lake City.

It was time to share my story.

————

And so, on a chilly Sunday evening in January, Gillian came over to our house and sat down in our living room with Sheina and me. She pulled out her phone.

"Are you okay if I record this?"

This was it. If I said yes, there was no turning back.

Is Gillian the reporter I trust?

Am I ready to share my story?

"Yes," I said. Then the questions began.

29

Mornings and Nights

February 4, 2019

Gillian interviewed me for three hours that first night and then wanted to come by my office for thirty minutes for some follow-up questions a few weeks later.

"My editors are really excited about this story," she said by way of introduction when she arrived at the synagogue. "They think it has tremendous potential, and they want to run it the day of the prelim."

At that point, I still thought we were months and months away from any sort of release date. Apparently, that timeline was now two weeks.

Gillian asked great questions.

She won my trust by helping me dig deep and process how I really felt about everything that had happened. Our thirty minutes of follow-up questions quickly turned into another three-hour conversation.

When she felt like she had what she needed, she thanked me for my time and got up to leave, but I had to double-check one more thing.

"So," I started, "I can still kill this if I want, right?"

She had made it clear that I didn't have the authority to make edits, but I just wanted to know if I could cut the whole thing if it came down to it.

"Yes, Avremi," she said. "I suppose you could technically do that."

Saying yes to Gillian and this story was like getting into a boat and heading off into the sea. I had set sail, and now the shore was a long way behind me, but I still wasn't quite ready to let go. I needed to know I could turn back if I changed my mind.

One last attempt to hold on to a little control.

―――――

A few evenings later, Sheina went out with some friends. I put the boys to bed and sat down in my living room by myself, mind racing.

Certainly I'm not the first person to go through this. I'm not the first male Orthodox survivor.

I wanted to know how the rest of the guys who went through this fared dealing with our community. Maybe they could offer some wisdom. So I pulled out my computer and Googled "male orthodox Jewish survivor of childhood sexual abuse."

Nothing.

Not one.

There were plenty of ex-orthodox survivors who came out and then torched the community. But there was not a single survivor who had stayed in.

No way.

I tried changing the order of the words, switched out phrases, and scoured the internet for something. Anything. I found nothing.

That was a lonely feeling. Google always has an answer for every question, but it didn't yield a single result for this.

Maybe my Rabbi was right. Perhaps this was a bad idea.

Then I had a thought. It was impossible, implausible, that I was the only male observant survivor. In fact, there were probably people who had done this same Google search and ended up feeling exactly how I felt right now. I was fully entitled to sit here and mope. But instead of loneliness, what if I interpreted this moment as a responsibility instead of a downer?

I felt the enormous picture of the Rebbe, Rabbi Menachem M. Schneerson peering over my shoulder in the background.

The Rebbe had a revolutionary philosophy.

He taught us to challenge the way we think about the voids we experience in life.

If you are living somewhere that has a thriving Jewish community, but you know of a place that longs for one but doesn't have it, that's a void. There are two ways to think about that void. You can either feel bad for them, or you can see it as an opportunity to do something about it.

Maybe the only reason you see voids in life is to step into them.

A few years earlier, I saw a void in Salt Lake City, and Sheina and I moved there to fill it. When my Google search yielded no results, I saw a void. The question became, what was I going to do about it?

Was this loneliness I felt a cause for despair? Or a reason for inspiration? Could it be that God was allowing me to do something new? To start something new?

The more I thought about it, the more I realized the answer. This was no time to mope. This was a time to step into the void. If there weren't any male observant Jewish survivors in the world, I would be the first.

I'd be the one who makes sure the next person to Google this doesn't feel alone.

———

A few days before the prelim, I got a text from Elizabeth.

> **Elizabeth:** *How are you feeling about testifying?*
> **Me:** *Not great.*
> **Elizabeth:** *Would it be helpful if I came to the prelim?*

I felt bad asking her to drive eight minutes to Starbucks. The prelim was in downtown Salt Lake City. There was no way I was going to ask her to drive an hour down the mountain at 8:30 in the morning.

> **Me:** *I would never ask you to do that.*
> **Elizabeth:** *You didn't. I offered.*
> **Me:** *I mean, it's Tuesday at 8:30 in courtroom W33, and it would mean the sun, the moon, and most of the stars if you were there.*

At this point, Gillian was a girl possessed. She loved the story, and so did her editors. We were texting daily and doing more interviews over the phone. Every time we spoke, she'd tell me how excited the whole *Deseret News* was to run it. Their expectations had a lot in common with my anxiety—both were incredibly high.

The day before the prelim, I went into the D.A.'s office to prep with Donna; met Spencer, Gillian's photographer, at the courthouse for some photos; and then drove thirty minutes down to Sandy to meet a kid for a Bar Mitzvah lesson.

I was a nervous wreck.

Tomorrow I'd testify in open court, and then my story, with my full name and picture, would be released to the public. A civil war raged in my mind, and it was getting too strong for me to keep driving. So I pulled over to the side of the highway, a maneuver I was getting a little too good at.

The story will help people.
But my kids will never get married.
The story will help people.
But people will say mean things in the comments.
The story will help people.
What does that even mean? Who will it help? Do I even care?
I'm twenty-seven years old. Why do I have to make this choice? Why am I between this rock and this hard place?

It was an impossible decision.

I envied every car that drove past me, knowing full well their lives were vastly simpler than mine. *That guy in the Toyota Camry, normal. The woman in the Honda Odyssey, normal. There goes the GMC guy, normal. And then there's me.*

Meanwhile, my typical Spotify playlist played in the background—Jewish music that I listen to when I drive. I had it on for background noise, a soundtrack to my low-grade anxiety infestation.

As I sat there weighing my options, a song caught my attention—Chapter 92 in Psalms.

להגיד בבוקר חסדך ואמונתך בלילות

"To proclaim Your kindness in the morning and our faith in You at night."

Those words spoke to me. They were what I needed to hear. According to the Psalmist, there are mornings—times of light, clarity, and certainty. In the mornings, we proclaim God's kindness.

But then there are also nights—times of darkness, confusion, and uncertainty. In the night, we may not feel the kindness, and we may not have much left to give. But we can have faith. Faith that if we just keep going through the night, the morning will come again.

I was in the night and didn't have much left to give, but I did have enough faith to let go. To stop trying to find an answer to this impossible conundrum. To drive forward through the night until the morning light began to dawn in the eastern sky.

———

Gillian called that night to walk me through the story, reminding me one last time before we started that I had no authority to change anything. Not the best way to start the conversation.

I was a nervous wreck.

When she read the article, it only got worse.

"Gillian, I'm not telling you what to do. You've made it clear I don't have that ability. But for God's sake, did you really have to go with all the most vulnerable, gut-wrenching, revealing quotes? This could've just been about the facts, you know, you could've just told them what happened."

"Avremi, remember. You don't get to make those decisions."

"I know," I said and hung up.

I was not excited about it and called my mom, needing to unwind with a little humor.

"Is everything okay?" she immediately asked, like one tends to do when they get a phone call past 9 p.m.

"You know, Mom, I've always wanted to yell this at someone and then hang up. And so let me just say this to you, 'I'LL SEE YOU IN COURT!'"

Then I hung up.

30

The Prelim

February 5, 2019

Several people offered to give me a ride to the preliminary hearing, but I insisted on driving myself.

I was about to testify in open court about years of abuse and the shame that followed. A shame that caused me to cut myself off from my friends and family and isolate myself. It only felt fitting to make that journey alone.

Prelims are just as crazy as initial appearances. We weren't the only ones told to show up to the courtroom at 8:30 a.m.; all the other local cases that needed their prelim knocked out today were there as well.

No order.

No seating arrangements.

There are no signs in the packed hallway that say "Team Avremi" on one side and then "Team Vina" down on the other. When my dad and I took a seat on a bench right outside the entrance, Vina and her family walked up and sat down about five feet away.

That's one of the odd dynamics about a courthouse. For as much order as judges demand within their courtrooms, the hallways are the Wild West. You share benches, bathrooms, and plenty of dirty looks with your opponents.

My dad and I sat directly across from Vina and her team, neither side making any attempt to avert their eyes. If looks could kill, there would have been corpses up and down the hallway.

Open hostility.

AirPods were my saving grace. Music was my sanctuary—a shelter in the middle of the storm.

That morning I was listening to another Hebrew prayer. This one was from a passage in Jeremiah about a voice of weeping coming from the heavens. The sound is Rachel crying tears for her children and the prophet promising Rachel her tears would be accepted and her kids would come home one day.

In the Book of Genesis, Rachel died on the side of the road, so instead of being granted burial with her husband, Jacob, they buried her right there. That burial wasn't just for convenience; it was providential. Generations later, after the destruction of the Temple, that was the road the Jewish people (her children) would take when they headed into exile.

In other words, Rachel was buried on the side of the road to give her children a place to pray along the way.

I always found so much significance in that idea because, as a survivor of childhood sexual abuse, you feel like you are on the side of the road. You feel cast aside. Historically, Rachel is the matriarch of the kids on the side of the road—for all the survivors of childhood sexual abuse.

The song itself is slow and mournful, but it's filled with passion, and when it crescendos at the end, a snare drum fades in with a steady beat, sounding almost like a military march, a war drum urging me forward.

It became an anthem for my fight. A reminder that although I never wanted this war, it's what I had to do—and Rachel had my back.

When the doors opened, my team quickly rushed to the front bench, taking the best seats like an eager family boarding a Southwest flight. I didn't want to sit around and watch all the other prelims; I just wanted to do what I needed to do and go home.

Getting the front row put us in a good spot to go first.

By 8:27 a.m. the courtroom was packed and the doors were shut. Everyone had their seats and sat back impatiently, waiting for the fireworks to begin. It occurred to me that I had no idea what these other cases were all about. Theirs may be tame; they may not have shown up today ready to march into battle. But if we went first, these other people would certainly get the price of their admission; they were in for a show.

Then the back door swung open and Elizabeth Smart walked into the courtroom, car seat in hand—her dad trailing close behind, followed by murmurs from people all over the courtroom.

There's a GIF of Vince Carter in the 2000 Slam Dunk Contest right after his legendary off-the-bounce, between-the-legs slam dunk—he looks right at the camera and announces, "It's over," signaling with his arms that the rest of the contestants can go home now.

That's how I felt when Elizabeth walked into the courtroom. She smiled and gave me a subtle wave, and that's all I needed.

It's over.

I can do this.

This is my moment.

———

Prelims don't happen in front of your judge. They happen in front of whichever judge is assigned to prelims that week. On February 5, 2019, that was Judge Blanch.

Courtroom W33.

Judge Blanch sat down and asked who would like to go first. Donna Kelly gave a stern nod to the defense counsel, and they spoke up first.

"Good morning, Your Honor. Would the court hear the Florreich case?"

"Is your client present?"

"Yes," they said, as Vina stood up and moved to the table between her team.

Meanwhile, Donna moved up to the prosecution table.

"Alright, Miss Kelly," Judge Blanch said. "Would you like to call your first witness?"

Donna stood a little straighter, looked Judge Blanch in the eyes, and said, "Your Honor, the people call Avrohom Zippel to the stand."

With that sentence, my life changed forever.

I stood up from my spot (the first chair on the first bench) and tried to hide that I was shaking like a leaf. I have no recollection of walking up front, taking the oath, and sitting in the witness booth.

No memory.

I know I took the oath. I must've. I just don't remember it. My mind was so focused on getting through this that it forgot to record the events.

Everything was going haywire. All my systems were lost. My heart was racing, my legs were shaking, and my hands were demanding to be told where to go.

The only instructions I got were, "The microphone should be about eight inches from your mouth."

What? I'm sorry, security confiscated my tape measure.

I'm not good at eyeballing distances when I am calm, cool, and collected, let alone when the world is spinning around me.

A few days earlier, someone gave me a helpful piece of advice. "Pour yourself a cup of water," they told me. There's a pitcher and a cup right by the witness stand, and completing a physical movement successfully grounds you in the moment.

So I tried it.

I made a quick blessing and took a sip of the water. It really did help. My hands, mouth, and mind all did their jobs.

Surely if we can successfully take a sip of water, we can testify in open court.

"Good morning," Donna said. "State your name for the record."

"Avrohom Zippel."

"And you live in Salt Lake County?"

"Yes."

And off we went.

She set the table quite methodically. You were homeschooled. There was a babysitter. There was an incident. She touched you inappropriately.

"Is the person in question in the courtroom today?"

"Yes, she is."

"Can you point her out for the record?"

Oh yeah, I'll point her out for the record.

That was the question I needed, the question that reminded me why I was doing all this. I sat up straighter in my chair, looked over to the defense table, and pointed right at her. There was nothing meek about it; I pointed and held my stare.

"Could you describe what she is wearing for the record?"

"A red jacket of sorts," I said, keeping my finger up as she squirmed in her seat.

Before the prelim, Annie kept reminding me I really couldn't mess this up. There was no jury at this point. I was just talking to the judge. This was a probable cause hearing, and 99.9 percent of them get bound over for trial, meaning the judge decides a trial is necessary.

Unless Donna and I screwed this up royally, we would walk out of this one with a win. Once Donna and I found our rhythm, being up there wasn't all that bad. She ended up asking me questions for about twenty-five minutes, then sat down.

"Cross?" Judge Blanch said, looking over at the defense table.

————

How are you supposed to feel about the people who are being paid to represent the person who ruined your life? I had grappled with that question since the first news release about Vina's arrest. It had included a small, innocent paragraph at the bottom, notifying the world that she was being represented by two attorneys. We'll call them Charlie and Joshua.

I'm grateful to live in the freest country in the world. I understand that living in that country affords Vina certain rights. I would want those same rights should I be in her shoes one day. I decided I'd wait and see how these guys acted before I formed an opinion.

Joshua forever gave off the impression of being an hour late and a dollar short. I Facebook stalked him at the outset and found out he was a symphony conductor as a hobby. The image of him with his eyes closed waving a baton is something I can never unsee, and I would have to withhold a chuckle each time he got up to speak in court.

Charlie was another story.

Charlie always came across like a grumpy grandpa who had been woken up from his afternoon nap for the family outing, only to find out that some of the kids hadn't used the bathroom yet or even packed their stuff. Jacket and pants never matched, tie always askew. To this day, I've never seen him crack a smile, not even in conversation with a colleague.

Typically, Joshua did all the speaking for Team Vina, and Charlie was there to give out dirty looks. But to my surprise, it was Charlie who rose for cross-examination.

As he stood up, I figured I was in the clear for the day. There was no jury to win over. Surely they'd save their hard-hitting questions for trial. But Charlie jumped right in, asking questions about my intent and bringing up that I was, at times, the one initiating the events in the latter half of the abuse.

There was no legal value to those questions. Every judge knows that even if a minor is the one to initiate a sexual encounter with an adult, it's still the adult's problem.

They weren't asking that question for the judge; they were asking it for me.

It was a scare tactic.

But their intimidation attempt had the opposite effect. It steadied my mind, narrowed my focus, and motivated me to stand my ground.

Okay, that's what we're doing? Do you want to get under my skin? I'll get under yours.

Thirty minutes later, Judge Blanch told me I could step down.

I grabbed my empty plastic cup and stepped off the stand.

The judge asked the defense if their client would testify. Upon hearing a stern *no*, Judge Blanch made a quick decision.

"Counsel, I have found the State has provided probable cause for the charges against the defendant, and your client is bound over for trial."

Another win!

Another out!

Of course this one was going to happen. But something about the judge saying it hit differently.

"In the future, the hearings will be held in front of Judge Trease. How soon would you like to see Judge Trease?"

"Well, Your Honor," Joshua started, pulling out his calendar as per usual. "I have so many cases stacked up right now. We're going to need some time."

We landed on a date at the beginning of March and were dismissed.

———

"What a moron," Detective Blue said loudly in the hallway. "What a moron. He just kept trying to dig you out, and instead, he handed you the shovel. What an idiot."

Amidst the chaos of the crowded hallway, Detective Blue and Donna were the only two people I had eyes for. I needed to know how I did.

"Don't sugarcoat it, Donna. How'd I do?"

"Not bad for your first time," she said with a calming smile.

Elizabeth was standing farther down the hallway, on the other side of the entrance. Right as we locked eyes, the doors to the courtroom flung open and Vina came strutting out between us, her entire entourage at her side. They were up in arms.

What did you think was going to happen?

All these cases get bound over. What did you think was going to happen?

You didn't even testify.

That was the first moment I wondered if they were getting some bad advice. It seemed like they went into each hearing being told the whole thing would get thrown out.

I'd learned by then to walk into every hearing with fair and balanced expectations and best- and worst-case scenarios. But it always seemed like they only showed up with high hopes and felt like the rug had just been pulled right out from under them.

I thanked Elizabeth for showing up and walked out of the courthouse. The sun was shining. The birds were chirping. It was a beautiful February morning.

I did it.

I testified.

I figured testifying was a lot like running a marathon. Incredibly difficult in the moment, but once you do it, you've done it. No one can take that away from you, and you'll never have to testify again for the first time.

———

Two really big things were happening that day; the prelim was just the first.

Gillian's story was scheduled to drop at 5 p.m., so I set an appointment with Dr. Michaels at 3:30 p.m. to debrief everything. Then I headed to the mall for a little retail therapy.

At 4:58 p.m., I was driving up 600 South and got a text from Gillian.

It's live.

I immediately took a hard right into the closest parking lot, a local soap shop called the Purring Buddha. After the world's fastest scan through the article, I got back on the road and sped off toward my office to post the story on my social media.

Even though that drive only took five minutes, I already had a text message when I arrived. The text was from a colleague of mine I had worked with on a project several years prior:

> Hi Avremi, I know it's been a while since we talked, but I just saw the Deseret News article. I just want to say I'm very grateful you would share your story.

We hadn't talked in years, and he reached out within three minutes.

That was a friendly reminder that the whole world now had access to my story, and it was just the beginning. For the next forty-eight hours, my phone did not stop buzzing.

The story went everywhere.

It spread like wildfire.

I left my phone on vibrate that night on purpose, waking up every few minutes to another buzz, another reminder from On High that I had done the right thing.

———

In Salt Lake City, we are usually good for one big snowstorm a year.

That night was our storm for the season.

We woke up to about eighteen inches of snow, but I needed the paper, so I put on my boots and marched down the road to 7-Eleven. I knew it would make the paper, but I wasn't expecting much. The State of the Union had also been that night, so I assumed I'd be playing second fiddle to a bunch of political ramblings.

The first thing I noticed when I walked into 7-Eleven and glanced at the newsstand was that the President's picture was pretty small for the morning after the State of the Union. It wasn't until I unfolded the paper that I realized why. I had the featured story, my picture front and center. The headline read "Stepping Out of the Shadows."

I couldn't believe it.

I reached for the copy below in case the top one had been one of my brothers playing a prank on me. It wasn't. My picture and my story were the featured story.

When I got home, Immanuel was the first one who wanted to see the paper. When the photographers had come to our home, he was old enough to understand what was going on.

"Did they put in all the pik-tos of me in the paper?"

I opened it up and showed him the spread. His eyes raced across the pages at both of his pictures that made it in.

"Two pik-tos of me!" he said with glee. "Okay, that's good."

And there it was.

The story was officially deemed acceptable by my three-and-a-half-year-old son.

Sheina is not active on social media, but the night before, she decided to share the story on her page, writing a beautiful paragraph to accompany it. That small gesture meant the world. Out of all the nice things people would say in the days to come, that paragraph held the most weight.

We stood there for a second, marveling at the story.

Celebrating how far we'd come.

Then we simultaneously realized we were out of diapers for our youngest. Such is the life of two young parents trying to make a difference in the world while raising two young kids at the same time.

I put my boots back on and headed out into the snow.

At this point, I had given up on trying to keep up with all the calls. But when I felt my phone vibrate again, I realized I had a moment in this slow trudge through the snow to answer this one.

"Hello."

"Rabbi Zippel?" a shaky voice said on the other line.

"Yes."

"You don't know me," he said through muffled tears. "Who I am is unimportant. I'm a Reform Rabbi, and I just wanted you to know that— that—"

He tried to catch his breath through all the tears.

"That your story is going to save lives."

He let out a sob and hung up.

———

The story spread like wildfire.

That week Gillian texted me to let me know the story got over 100,000 page views. It would go on to become the most viewed page on the *Deseret News* in its time.

On Friday morning, I was informed Aly Raisman had retweeted the story:

> *Wow. Thanks for your bravery and courage Rabbi Zippel. You will inspire so many others to share their stories. Thank you for speaking your truth! I support you.*

For years, I had agonized over being the survivor of sexual abuse, as if that was the only thing I could be known for. And you know what? I was right. That's exactly what happened. That was quickly becoming my identity, the thing that would be attached to me from then on out.

But the thing that made all the difference had nothing to do with how other people perceived me and had everything to do with how I perceived myself.

I had accepted I was a survivor of childhood sexual abuse.

That was my story.

And if talking about my journey could help other people with theirs, then I decided I wasn't just going to talk; I was going to shout.

31

Wants and Needs

April 2019

"We need to talk."

It was Annie. She called to ask if I'd be willing to come by her office to have what she called "a very important conversation."

The topic was my *wants* versus my *needs*.

It was time for us to sit down and have an honest conversation about separating the two. The trial was going to be brutal, and defense counsel made sure to remind us of that as often as they could.

Part of the game between the prosecutor and the defendant is both sides being open to finding some compromises—some middle ground.

Annie knew there might be opportunities in the near future to find some common ground with the defense counsel and settle in a way that made both sides happy. In order to do that, my team had to know what I needed out of this whole thing. To get there, we had to separate which things were luxuries that I wanted and which ones were non-negotiables that I needed.

———

In 2014, Sheina and I drove from Brooklyn to Toronto for the first anniversary of my Zaidy's death. While driving home through upstate New York, I got the biggest speeding ticket of my life.

Ninety-six in a 70—26 mph over the speed limit.

Fortunately, there's a big market for traffic lawyers in that part of the state because drivers around there speed like crazy. I was not the first nor would I be the last person to go through this process.

The ticket was not cheap.

"Look," the attorney said, "the ticket is $450, and because you were so high over the speed limit, it's about six points on your license. Here's how I need you to think about it; either way, that $450 is gone. You'll never see it again. But instead of paying the court the money, pay it to me, and I will negotiate the ticket down so you don't get points on your license."

"Fair enough," I said. That wasn't the news I hoped to hear, but it was my best option. A week later, I got an email from the attorney asking me to sign a plea that said I was pleading guilty to running a stop sign.

Apparently, his negotiation tactic was to bring it down from speeding twenty-six miles over the speed limit to running a stop sign.

I was royally confused.

"Look, I'm happy to do whatever you want," I told him. "But how can I sign this? It's a blatant lie. There was no stop sign involved."

"That's how it works," he said calmly. "The court signed off; just sign it."

I signed the plea, got no points on my license, and never heard from him again.

————

Plea deals are gymnastics—legal gymnastics.

As I thought through my wants and needs, one thing was clear. My biggest need was to ensure Vina would not win a gold medal in legal gymnastics. Aly Raisman wins the gold medals in gymnastics—let's leave that to her. I needed this to be different than my speeding ticket, and I needed Vina to admit she really had abused me.

In Utah, sexual abuse of a child is only a second-degree felony. However, there are aggravating circumstances that bump it up to a first-degree felony. The most common is when the person who commits a crime is in a position of power.

Vina was charged with aggravated sexual abuse of a child because she was a person of power in my life.

For me, the jump from second-degree to first-degree was extra meaningful. Her position of power is the reason it happened; it's why she was able to manipulate me in the first place.

So what was my need?

I needed Vina to plead guilty to one first-degree felony, to one count of aggravated sexual abuse of a child. No legal gymnastics. Admit that she, as a person of power in my life, sexually abused me. That's what I needed.

Wants? Sure, I had lots of wants. But I made it clear to Annie that I had one need.

I wasn't out for vengeance; I didn't need painful punishment.

In fact, I told Annie that if Vina would plead guilty to one count of aggravated sexual abuse of a child, then I would go to sentencing and urge the judge and the Board of Pardons (the ones who ultimately have the authority to decide the length of a sentence in Utah) to only keep her in for three years.

That's it.

I would ask for it personally.

But—and this was crucial—I needed her to accept and admit what she'd done. I needed her to be accountable for one count—just one. Pick any one of the seven, and plead guilty, and we will call it a day.

That sounded more than reasonable to me.

Annie talked to Donna and Amy, and together, they presented the offer to the defense counsel. We didn't have to wait long for a response. They turned it down immediately.

They didn't even consider it.

They didn't offer a counter.

Nothing.

———

The disposition hearing happened at the beginning of April. At a disposition, the judge finally sets forth the game plan and schedule for trial.

On either side of every courtroom, there is a small conference room you can use for private conversations. I always thought of them as closets. When we arrived for the disposition, Donna went into one such closet to have a conversation with the defense counsel. This particular closet had windows looking into the courtroom, so although you couldn't hear them, you could see them.

I sat back and watched, making no attempt to avert my eyes when they'd glance over at me. Charlie was animated. They spoke the entire time while Donna sat back and listened.

After the meeting, Donna came into the courtroom, and for the first time in almost a year that I had known her, she made a snide comment. "Well, I was just lectured to," she said, shaking her head. "And I made sure to thank them for providing me with their closing argument."

The defense counsel had just spent the last seven minutes warning Donna not to let this go to trial. If it did, they threatened to make the case that the witness was a boy king who subjected their client to the most egregious sexual horrors and was just using her as the victim of all his sexual desires.

She walked away angry, and I sat there anxious.

Well, I guess that's how this is going to go.

———

"Counsel," Judge Trease said, "has any agreement been reached between the parties?"

"No, Your Honor," Donna replied, a little sharper than normal.

"Okay, we're going to calendar this for trial."

"Yes, Your Honor, we anticipated that," Joshua said, jumping to his feet. "We'd ask the court to provide us five days for trial. We feel there is lengthy evidence to sort through, and we will have a number of expert witnesses to call."

"Five days?" Judge Trease responded.

"Yes, Your Honor."

Unless it's murder, most trials last one to two days. Five days is almost unheard of.

"Well, the soonest I can schedule a five-day trial is the end of October."

I'm sorry. Did she say the end of October? It's April.

"Thank you, Your Honor."

Then Judge Trease turned her attention to Vina. "Ma'am, you have a constitutional right to a speedy trial. By asking for a five-day trial, you are effectively waiving your right to your speedy trial. Are you aware of that?"

Vina looked at her with a blank stare.

"Ma'am, do you understand what I am saying?"

Nothing.

"Counsel," Trease continued, "does your client struggle to understand English?"

They jumped all over that opportunity. "Yes, Your Honor. She does. We ask for an interpreter to be appointed for all further hearings."

Donna had a confused look on her face.

"Okay," Trease said. "The trial is set for the end of October, and there will be an interpreter there."

We weren't mad about that; we were confused. Especially since there was a long recorded phone call of Vina speaking English that would be played at the trial.

Whatever.

———

Waiting until October wasn't ideal, but it also didn't get to me the way it would've six months earlier.

I was growing.

I was letting go of control.

Plus, I now had a life outside of this. Gillian's story opened doors for me to step into the world of advocacy. I was working with a bunch of survivors and their families and had opportunities to sit down with people to help them process their own situations, and for the first time in a long time, I felt like I was playing offense, not just defense.

———

At the beginning of June, I was on a field trip with our Hebrew School kids when I got an email from Annie informing me the defense counsel had filed a motion to delay the trial indefinitely. Apparently, a bunch of "stuff" had come up, and they needed to push things back.

A hearing was set for June 24.

That was the first day of our summer camp at the synagogue, one of the days of the year I couldn't miss. That would be the only hearing I didn't show up for. My parents went in my place.

They called me an hour after the hearing, giddy.

Since it was a newly requested hearing, defense counsel told Vina she didn't need to be in court—wrong move.

"Where's your client?" Trease asked when the hearing began.

"She's not here," they said.

"What do you mean she's not here? She's out on bail. Do I need to revoke her bail?"

They went on to explain they were under the impression she didn't need to be there, and Judge Trease was livid. "You don't have the authority to decide that," she said. "Your client is out on bail. She must be at every hearing. Now, why are we here? What's your motion?"

The defense counsel went on to explain they needed the trial pushed back and made their case. Annie told me after the hearing that Judge Trease stopped them in their tracks at that moment and ripped them a new one with some choice words. Of all the moments I had to miss, I couldn't believe I missed that one. It would've done my heart good.

The hearing ended with Trease moving the trial back two weeks to a shorter four-day week. Monday, November 11, was Veteran's Day, and the court would be closed, so the trial would run for four days—from Tuesday, November 12 to Friday, November 15.

That was it.

No more games.

No more changes.

Come hell or high water, the trial would begin on November 12.

32

The Countdown
to Trial

Summer 2019

In the leadup to trial, Judge Trease set a hearing for mid-August for both sides to present their lists of evidence and witnesses. The night before the pretrial hearing was the Utah vs. BYU football game. When those two teams play each other, every single person in the state of Utah is either red (Utah) or blue (BYU). There is no purple—no one is neutral.

It is very binary.

Pick a side.

I felt the same way when I walked into the pretrial hearing the following day. This hearing wasn't part of a motion calendar. There was no one else in the courtroom.

Vina's team was there.

My team was there.

Judge Trease was there.

That's it.

The two sides were very clearly defined and dug in. You were either red or you were blue—no purple allowed.

The point of the pretrial hearing was to ensure both sides were clear and okay with the evidence and witness lists the other side would be bringing to the table. The defense counsel had talked about a long list of expert witnesses and filed a long list of motions.

On paper, their case was impressive.

But as Judge Trease started going through the motions one by one, the defense counsel began "respectfully withdrawing the motion."

Then Judge Trease would read the next one, and the same thing would happen.

One after the next after the next.

When it came down to it, their long list of motions, evidence, and expert witnesses seemed more like a bluff than a reality.

Meanwhile, Donna was sitting back with a slight smile on her face. The longer I got to know her and watch her in action, the more my trust and appreciation for her rose. She knew what she was doing the whole time. Surrounded by a bunch of people playing checkers, Donna was always playing chess.

———

That September, Chanel Miller's book *Know My Name* came out.

Chanel's story is heartbreaking.

She is the girl who was raped on the Stanford campus in 2016. When the perpetrator was found guilty and sentenced to prison, his father wrote in a letter, "That is a steep price to pay for 20 minutes of action out of his 20 plus years of life."

Chanel stayed anonymous throughout the whole process. She was Jane Doe until she released her book with a fitting title.

This book was the first time she ever came forward and told her story. It's breathtakingly beautiful, gut-wrenchingly sad, and deeply vulnerable all at the same time. I picked it up during a Jewish holiday and couldn't put it down.

She wrote about how the defense counsel spoke about the rape as if it were something that "just happened." They'd talk about how sad it was that this thing happened to her and then immediately jump to how bad the sentencing was for their client.

As if the two were equal.

But they weren't—one caused the other. And until both sides can admit that, it doesn't feel much like justice for the victim.

She talked about how offended she was by that.

The way we talk about this stuff really does matter.

Chanel put language to the way I was feeling, and I'll forever be grateful for that.

My phone was turned off that day for the holiday. When I turned it on, I had an email from Annie. She was forwarding an email from Donna, who was forwarding an email from the defense counsel.

They wanted a deal.

They wanted a compromise.

They wrote out a long email ending with:

> **We recognize that Mr. Zippel has gone through a lot, and we want a resolution that will give him closure and a sense that justice is done. We also want a resolution where in Ms. Florreich can live out what is left of her life with her family. It seems to me, that the stakes are high for all concerned at trial. And perhaps this isn't a case any of us really want to play out in the courtroom....as far as sentencing, she has already acknowledged to us that a long probation and house arrest is definitely on the table.**

"Mr. Zippel has gone through a lot."

The words jumped off the page and seared themselves onto my mind.

No, no, no.

Do you know who has gone through a lot? Someone whose house burned down. Someone who got sick. Someone whose business collapsed in the middle of the night. Those are people who have gone through a lot. "Gone through a lot" is a really great way to make someone's misfortune sound ambiguous.

I haven't "gone through a lot." I was sexually abused by your client.

Chanel Miller was right; we need to start calling it what it is.

We can't just throw out ambiguous phrases and sweep the fallout under the rug.

We have to give them a name.

We have to be honest.

Until we do, we will continue sending a message to possible future perpetrators that this behavior is tolerable.

Annie's email to Donna and the defense counsel summed up my stance well:

> **Hello, both of you. As the two parties of this case discuss this matter, this is the need of Mr. Zippel. He wants Ms. Florreich to acknowledge, admit, and accept responsibility for her actions and for her sexual abuse of him as a child. The specifics of which he testified to at the preliminary hearing. That is all he wants. That is what he needs. No sugarcoating. No "legal fictions."**

They wanted legal gymnastics. But we weren't having it. That's not what we were doing here.

And yet, we were well aware that they were sending us a warning shot. They ended their email with, "This is not a case that either one of us wants to play out in a courtroom." At that point, I knew Vina had already freely thrown out the term "rape." She had no qualms about trying to flip the script and accuse me.

This was war.

And so we got ready for trial.

———

As the trial got closer, all the maturity and growth I felt left me.

The trial consumed me.

October 31 was the date we set for witness prep. The court was closed that day, so Donna didn't have any cases, and I don't celebrate Halloween, so it was the perfect day.

My mom and I went to the D.A.'s office together.

Donna wanted to call my mom up on the stand as the first witness at trial for two reasons.

First, in the police report, Detective Blue had written that in his interview with my mother, she had reacted with "disbelief." The defense counsel jumped all over that, trying to twist those words to make it sound like my mom's disbelief was directed toward me—that she thought I was lying. Donna wanted to let my mom clarify what anyone with any bit of critical thinking skills knew—the disbelief was directed toward Vina, not me.

Second, Donna wanted my mom to set the scene for what the household was like. She wanted her to help the jury understand the standards of Judaism in our home and how important modesty is to us. We needed to show that Vina knew all about our values, because the trial was going to come down to one thing: sexual intent. Donna wanted to prove that Vina knew this was absolutely inappropriate behavior.

Once my mom finished her prep, she headed out.

Which was wise. Her hour of prep was really emotional for both of us. Reality was setting in that this would be an emotional roller coaster for my whole family. The prelim had just been about hitting the high notes, but now it was time to take the court through the entire story.

No amount of therapy could prepare me for the next several hours.

The conference room on the third floor is all glass. As we prepped, I could see everything happening in the D.A.'s office. They were having an office-wide Halloween party. Adorable little kids decked out in full costumes were working their way up and down the hallways, hauling in as much candy as they could.

The dichotomy was too much to handle.

Outside the conference room, kids were living the epitome of childhood innocence. They were putting costumes on and asking strangers for candy, blissfully ignorant of the evils of the world. Meanwhile, inside the conference room, I was sitting with my attorneys, outlining a childhood filled with torturous shame and self-loathing.

There were two giant whiteboards in the room. As we talked, Donna completely filled both. The whiteboards helped us see the pattern. The evolution of the events. The progressive worsening of each incident.

The pattern did something to me.

Even after all my sessions with Dr. Michaels, I couldn't contain myself.

It was all up there.

None of this was what I was expecting in life.

"Let's take a break," Donna said, sensing the heaviness in the room.

I collapsed into my chair and could feel myself coming back into my body as if I had left it for the last two and a half hours. Two truths hit me at the same time: I needed to use the restroom and I was about to pass out from hunger.

As I got up to go to the bathroom, it occurred to me that when a trauma survivor remembers an event, they really do detach. They leave behind the scarred body that's been through hell and go to a place where they cease to feel bodily functions.

When I got back, Donna had a mound of Guava Laffy Taffys on the desk—the only Kosher snack in the entire office.

"Thanks, Donna," I said, offering the closest thing to a smile I could muster.

We prepped for another hour and then called it quits.

Sheina asked me how it went when I got home, and she could tell how emotionally drained I was. "Look," I told her, "there's a lot of information that is going to be talked about at trial. No details are going to be spared. I'd understand if you don't want to be there."

She appreciated the sentiment and told me she'd think about it. But we both knew there wasn't much debate in her mind; she wasn't going to miss it.

———

There were a lot of things I wanted to do in the week leading up to the trial, but only one thing I knew I had to do—hang out with Elizabeth.

She invited me to her home the week before, and we sat and talked for two hours. She told me about her experiences in trial—all the frustrating moments, the scary moments, and the hopeful moments. It was the most therapeutic thing I could've done. I didn't leave with a long list of "the do's and don'ts for trial." I left with something much better. I left knowing I had a friend who understood what I was going through.

I spent the day before trial teaching a Bar Mitzvah lesson in Lehi. As I was about to get back on the highway to make the forty-five-minute drive up to Salt Lake City, I received an email from Donna with the subject line: **Tomorrow**.

The email was well beyond her job description and summed up the journey we'd been on brilliantly.

> **I am at my office, obsessively reviewing things for the millionth time. And just wanted to send you all a note to let you know I am feeling great about this case and this trial. We have a great and fair judge who doesn't put up with nonsense. We have a defendant who is trying to fool the jury to believe that she doesn't**

understand English or that she was intimidated by the police or that she was perved on by an eight-year-old child. The jury is going to see right through it for the BS that it is. And we have a nightmare victim—truthful, kind, and honest to a fault. Whatever happens, Avremi, please know that I believe you and am ready to fight for justice for you. Sleep well tonight, friends. Tomorrow is our day.

Tomorrow is our day.

Yes, the trial was about Vina, but Donna was reminding me that this was my day. It was my chance to push back against the narrative that wanted to sweep sexual abuse under the rug.

This was my opportunity to tell my story.

33

The Jury

November 15, 2019
1:11 p.m.

The courtroom has never looked this clean.

Four days earlier, the tables had stacks and stacks of paperwork—the culmination of countless hours of emails, phone calls, and meetings during this two-year investigation. Over the last four days, we slowly inched our way through every single paper.

Statements.

Witnesses.

Questions.

Evidence.

Objections.

The accusations have been made. The institutions have been instituted. Mud has been flung. I glance over at the bare surface of the defendant's table and then at the prosecutor's table. All the papers are gone, the evidence removed; the courtroom is clean.

We've made it through trial.

And the jury has heard it all. Nine strangers, missing work, canceling plans, being away from their families, to sit in this courtroom and listen to my story.

We rise to our feet as they enter. They have certainly gotten their steps in, constantly being asked to enter and then leave.

In and out.

In and out.

This will be their final entrance—they have the verdict in hand.

Just four days ago, fifty potential jurors sat around the courtroom, wondering what type of case was about to unfold. Forty-one went home early; the other nine certainly got a show. I doubt they expected any of this when they got that notorious summons to jury duty in the mail.

Reading Donna's email that Monday on the way back from the Bar Mitzvah lesson felt like a lifetime ago—*tomorrow is our day.* She was right. The last four days may not have gone how I expected, and I'm happy to never have to live them again, but I finally had my day in court.

Now, everything comes down to the nine humans taking their seats in the jury box.

34

Trial (Day One)

November 12, 2019

I skipped breakfast that morning.

To be fair, skipping breakfast indicated that my days and nights followed some sort of pattern. Sleep for several hours during the night, awake when it's light, and eat three square meals a day—one in the morning, one in the afternoon, and the last in the evening. But nothing could be further from the truth. Any semblance of rhythm and routine was out the window, and it had been for quite some time.

Whatever it took, some form of me would get to trial.

Trial.

The word danced on my tongue in the shower, with all of the ironies contained therein—the highest point of our justice system. The day a jury of our peers would decide right from wrong.

I dressed in the dark and let Sheina hang on to whatever vestiges of sleep she'd been attempting to cling to. The night before, I had laid out the gray suit and black polka-dotted tie.

The irony made me chuckle.

The eight or nine strangers of the jury were about to hear the most sordid details of my life, and I was busy wondering if they'd like the patterns on my tie.

I drove to Chabad and relished the opportunity to recite my morning prayers quietly. God and I needed to have a powwow before I headed downtown, and I knew exactly what I needed to ask for.

Peace of mind.

The ability to focus.

A clear head.

And an ability to maintain some semblance of control over my emotions.

———

When I got back from the synagogue, Spenser greeted me on my doorstep.

Of all the reactions I thought having a camera follow me to the courthouse would have, calming was not one of them. My boys greeted us as we popped inside to grab my stuff and finally head to court.

In the eighteen months I had been making the trek to the Matheson Courthouse, I had always insisted on going alone, often to my parents' chagrin. I needed those rides. They were my time to blast the music, get my head right, and map out the ways that hearing could be our finest hour or greatest tragedy.

Today was the exception to the rule. My mother made it clear to me that as much as she respected my ritual, there was no way any son of hers was going to trial on his own.

We compromised.

My mother got in the passenger seat, and Spenser jumped in the back, trusted camera in hand. He was the one to break the silence as we turned onto 700 East.

"So how are you feeling, Avremi?"

How am I feeling? Where should I start?

"Honestly, most of all relieved and grateful," I said, thankful for the opportunity to articulate some emotions. "I know there are so many survivors out there, the overwhelming majority wish for this opportunity and never get it, and honestly, I just want my day in court. I want to say my piece, unencumbered, and let everyone do with that whatever they please."

I meant every word.

My typical routine was going to feel a little different with two other people in the car, but they'd manage. If there was one day of my life that my mother wouldn't grimace at the volume of the music, I was sure going to take advantage of it. As we pulled up to the D.A.'s office, I blasted "Tatty, My King" as loud as the speakers would let me.

> I'm starting to realize
> that You've held me so tight
> I'll follow your plan
> Just don't let go of my hand.

Faith was all I had, but maybe faith was all I needed.

Donna and Annie were already inside. Amy was waiting to walk me in.

Team Avremi.

There was less small talk than usual and a heightened focus in their eyes. This was game day, and we were ready.

"Front door or back door?" Amy asked as we made the short walk to the courthouse.

"I'm sure there will be times I'll just wanna slip in the back, but while I can, let's go through the main entrance," I answered.

The revolving doors of the Matheson Courthouse spun us into the usual 8 a.m. rush. The typical stares that followed my black hat were compounded by the man with a video camera walking with me, but I couldn't care less.

I got my ritual wink from the lady at the information desk and turned to Amy. "I'm missing my gym over the next couple of days, so I'm taking the stairs."

"Great idea," she responded.

You've got to love a county-appointed social worker. If I had suggested going up while standing on my head, she probably would've joined me with a smile.

The stairwell was what I had hoped it would be—cool and quiet.

My tempo was slow and steady, the clicks and clacks of my dress shoes matching the mantra of my thoughts: *You control exactly nothing once you get upstairs. Fight for yourself, one breath at a time.*

The door to the fourth-floor hallway swung open, and the west wing beckoned.

I walked down to the end of the hallway, where the bird statue marked the doors to my home over the next few days.

W49.

The courtroom of Judge Vernice Trease.

Six hundred sixty-five days after a cold call to the Salt Lake City Police Department, against the most improbable of odds, the State of Utah was taking Alavina Florreich to trial.

———

When we first entered the courtroom, there was little to no law or order.

The attorneys were called back into chambers with Judge Trease, and the rest of us were sitting around like a bunch of elementary school kids after the teacher walked out of the room, except this classroom was very clearly divided between two sides that hated each other. And to make it worse, there was a guy I had never met staring at me. I locked eyes with him, trying to give him a stern warning, but he wouldn't look away.

It's one thing to catch someone looking at you, but when you make eye contact with them and they refuse to look away, it leaves a bad feeling.

Great, I guess I'm going to have some unnamed guy I've never seen shooting me death stares from across the room all week.

———

First up on the docket, jury selection.

Fifty potential jury members sat in the courtroom, fulfilling their civic duties. Most of them were nodding off to sleep through the standard announcements that begin jury selection, at least until Judge Trease explained that the defendant, Alavina Florreich, was charged with five first-degree felonies of aggravated sexual abuse of a child and two second-degree felonies of forcible sexual abuse of a minor.

The jury sat at attention.

Every eye had shifted to the defendant's table. I watched them try to solve the riddle before them. There are three people sitting at that table, and two of them have stacks of paper in front of them, so who's left? The woman?

Eyes widened.

Mouths opened.

Confusion all over their faces.

My mind was racing.

Not a single one of them can believe it.

They aren't going to put a sweet seventy-year-old woman in prison.

We're doomed.

How are we going to do this?

For a criminal case, you need eight jurors and one alternate. We needed to whittle fifty potential jurors down to nine.

The questions began.

Trease asked if anyone knew Vina or me, and when their eyes scanned over to me, their already confused faces became even more so.

He's a grown man?

When she asked if anyone had any personal proximity to sexual abuse of a child, twenty numbers went up into the air. (Potential jurors are given numbers at the start of trial that the officials can use to identify them.)

One by one, Trease called their numbers and asked them to elaborate.

Each person had their own unique situation, their own heartbreak, their own story. As we went through person by person, the tears began to flow.

One juror told a story about a math teacher.

Another juror broke down as she explained what happened to her daughter.

The atmosphere in the room completely shifted—and so did the trial.

Even the people who didn't have their cards up were profoundly impacted. People don't make this stuff up.

Over the next few days, the defense counsel's biggest angle was going to be that I was doing this all for publicity. But the tears of the dismissed jurors would linger in that room for the next four days, washing away those lies and reminding each one of us of the profound pain sexual abuse leaves on its victims.

When Judge Trease asked if anyone had come across news coverage of this case, one guy slowly and shyly raised his hand and explained that his girlfriend had sent it to him. He was shy, and it was obvious there was a part of him that didn't want to say what he knew he needed to say next: "She thought it might help me."

Another dagger.

He was excused, and I wished I could run down and hug him.

Slowly but surely, fifty became nine.

Before we were dismissed for lunch, we had our jury.

———

We all got back from lunch, and things settled down a little.

I claimed what no one would argue was my rightful seat for the week—the first chair in the first row. Annie and Amy sat next to me, and Sheina and my mother sat next to them. My father was, and would remain, in the seat directly behind me for the entirety of trial—never in my way, but never too far away either.

On the other side of the bar, Donna took her seat at the prosecutor's table. Detective Blue would be joining her soon.

Across the aisle, Charlie and Joshua were on either side of their client. Vina sat at the defendant's table with large headphones covering her ears. Meanwhile, two interpreters were seated a few feet to her left. They would take turns translating every word of the trial into Tongan for Vina for the next four days.

With my peripheral vision, I did my best to make out the family and friends sitting behind Vina. But I kept my gaze straight ahead, figuring there would be plenty of dirty looks thrown across the aisle over the next few days and wanting to hold off from breaking down that barrier for as long as possible. It felt like we were two armies marching toward each other, and even though the end result was inevitable, I could hold off on launching an arrow for as long as possible.

Then Judge Trease entered her courtroom.

———

There's a blessing we make in my community whenever we do something time-connected.

> Blessed are you, Lord our God, King of the Universe, who
> has enabled us to reach this occasion, who has kept us to
> this day.

We make that blessing on every holiday and every special occasion; it's our way of marking the moment.

We also make it every time we put on a new garment of clothing, because God is the one who sustained us to that day where we could own this new jacket or pants.

Before trial, I bought four new shirts because I wanted to make that blessing four times, at four different moments of the process.

As Judge Trease welcomed everyone and read the fifteen minutes of prewritten statements that every judge starts trials with, I whispered the first one quietly to myself. Like a professional athlete during the national

TRIAL (DAY ONE)   183

anthem, I closed my eyes and thanked God for enabling me to reach this occasion. It was only His strength that had gotten me there, and acknowledging that and feeling a sense of gratitude felt like the right way to start.

In court, there are a lot of rules and regulations you have to get used to.

For example, the exclusionary rule: The exclusionary rule states that those who are subpoenaed to testify in a criminal case aren't allowed to be there during the rest of the trial because they don't want something you hear to taint the accuracy of your testimony.

This makes logical sense when you think about it with no emotional attachment, but when your son is the victim of a crime, being told you aren't allowed to sit in the courtroom doesn't go over very well.

Since my mother was set to testify, Judge Trease asked her to leave before the opening statements began. That did not sit well with her. "Walk" would not be the correct word to explain what happened next; my mother stomped out, making it clear to everyone that she was not okay with being asked to leave.

Her reaction made me smile slightly. The whole "don't show emotion" thing isn't really her brand.

Once my mother left, we all stood to our feet as the jury entered the courtroom. The rules were set. The court was ready. It was time for the trial to begin.

Before we sat down, Donna turned around and reached into her pocket. She pulled out a Guava Laffy Taffy and placed it in my hands.

That meant the world to me. To this day, Donna and I still give presentations together. We give a number of talks, and one of them is about the craft of being a prosecutor. We explain the importance of prosecutors seeing their clients as human beings—individuals who have needs, wants, ups, and downs.

We call the presentation "Guava Laffy Taffys."

———

Donna went first.

She rose to her feet for her opening statement, and I leaned back in my chair, waiting for the fireworks to begin. But there weren't any. The statement fell flat. It's not that there was anything wrong with it; there just weren't any zingers.

No one-liners.

No mic-drop moments.

It felt lackluster.

Joshua, on the other hand, took the opposite approach. He stood up and made an opening statement infused with passion. It was personal. It was animated.

It made Vina look like a misunderstood saint.

It made me look like a clout-chasing liar.

He talked about the "privilege" that it was to represent Vina. He wanted the jury to know that she had emigrated to the United States from Tonga. I wasn't sure what that had to do with anything at all. I was going to lean forward and tell Donna that I emigrated to the United States from Toronto if anyone was curious.

He told stories of people who have used the #MeToo movement to gain followers and accused me of doing the same thing. They made it clear that they would prove that this was my fault—that Vina was preyed upon.

Are they really going to try to flip this whole thing?

I was eight.

Thank God my mom's not in here.

She would've bristled at their opening statement. I'm not sure she would've been able to keep quiet.

It was clear to me and everyone else in the room that they won the opening statements, like a team running out onto the floor and going on a commanding 10-0 run to begin the game.

My optimism was waning.

———

After the opening statements, it was our time to present our case. Donna called her first witness—my mother.

She walked in fuming with such emotion on her face that Judge Trease asked her if she was okay. For several weeks, Donna had been telling us my mother going first was strategic for the case. As she walked in, I wondered for the first time if maybe Donna was just trying to help my mother get back into court as quickly as possible—one mother to another.

For the next seventeen minutes, Donna asked the questions they had rehearsed, and my mom articulated what our house was like during those years. She helped the jury understand Judaism a little better, highlighting that Vina knew full well what she was doing was wrong on several levels. As they talked, you could see subtle nods begin to start from the jury. We never feel much pressure to explain our lifestyle to strangers, but if there were ever nine people we needed to understand us, these were them.

"No further questions, Your Honor," Donna said, satisfied with the ground they covered in such a short period of time.

"Cross-examination?" Trease asked.

When Charlie stood up for the cross, my mother looked him dead in the eye. They exchanged one of the heaviest, most intense stares I've ever seen between two people. "Animosity" is probably the right word, but it still falls short of describing the nonverbal feelings exchanged between the two.

He asked the strangest questions. They were small, detail-oriented questions that had little to nothing to do with the case. It felt like he was just trying to catch her in her words and get her to say something on the record they could take out of context. But then he asked my mother if she knew what actually went on in that downstairs bathroom, and the temperature in the room changed.

"No."

"You don't?" he asked again.

"I don't. And I don't want to know."

"So," Charlie continued, slowing down and trying to sound suspicious, "you have no idea what happened between the defendant and your son?"

The emotion was stirring up inside her as he asked one more time.

"To this day, you have no idea any of the details?"

That's when my mom landed the first right hook of the trial. She blurted out, "I know she told him he had a very big dick." She choked back an audible sob as she answered.

For context, one day my mother and I were driving home, and I told her the real reason I wanted this to go to trial was because I wanted the recorded phone call to be played in court. For everyone to hear.

"Why?" she asked me curiously. "What did she say?"

I tried to change the subject, but my mom wasn't having it.

"Mom," I finally told her, "she told me how big I was. She literally told me I have a big dick."

That was the end of that conversation. We never talked about it again—until she blurted that out from the stand.

The courtroom went silent.

That was the first sexual reference in trial.

The emotion in her voice made her sound like a wounded lioness, a mother having to sit through her child's pain.

Charlie was not expecting that; he didn't have a follow-up. While he stumbled about, trying to figure out how to respond, that comment took up residence in the courtroom.

It sat in the room.

Then he went right back into the weeds, asking more nitpicky follow-up questions to his already nitpicky questions.

———

Then it was my turn. My mom walked off the stand, and I intercepted her right in front of the jury box. I hugged her and kissed her right cheek as I whispered very clearly, "You did a great job."

Everyone on the jury heard me, by design.

Nine months ago, I zoned out on my way up to the stand. This time, I made myself at home and calmly fiddled with the microphone for no other reason than to show everyone how confident I was.

At this point, there were only forty-five minutes left in the day.

Most of my time on the stand would be reserved for day two, but with the few minutes we did have, Donna introduced our first piece of evidence—the floor plan of the basement.

Donna blew up the blueprint and put it right in front of the jury so everyone could get a visual representation of the events.

With Donna's questions as my jumping-off point, I started telling the jury everything. I explained how secluded the downstairs bathroom was from the rest of the house, how my siblings would've had to venture from their playroom and weave around the entire basement to ever catch us in the act.

I brought them into that dark, lonely basement and told them about the shame, regret, confusion, and self-hatred I felt there. I told my story to the best of my ability. As real and authentic as I knew how.

And then day one of trial ended.

———

"What are your thoughts?" Donna asked in her office during the debrief.

"Pretty much exactly what we had planned for," I said, but I couldn't help myself from bringing up the opening statements. "But, Donna, your opening statement wasn't quite what I expected."

She didn't get mad.

She didn't get defensive.

She didn't react—she just calmly responded.

"Years ago, when I was first starting out, I had a mentor," she explained. "I always used to ask what he was going to say in his opening statements, and he'd always shrug and tell me he never made big promises up top. He had no idea what he was going to prove during trial, and you don't want to disappoint the jury—trial is about the slow build."

Time would prove her wise.

The defense counsel's case would soon run out of steam; ours was just getting started.

———

When I got home, every part of my body was worn out. My legs felt like I had just run a marathon, my lungs felt like I had just climbed Everest, and my arms felt like I had been in the gym all day.

I sat down on the couch, overwhelmed by the reality that we were only 25 percent of the way through. Around 9 p.m., my phone pinged, signaling the coverage of the trial by the local papers. I had just finished skimming the articles when I found an email from a name that grabbed my attention.

> **Avremi, I can only imagine how difficult this trial is for you. Please know there are many of us who know you and admire the good you bring to our community. Thank you for having the courage to raise your voice for the good of others. You are in my thoughts and prayers. You have my support. I respect your bravery and integrity.**
>
> **United States Congressman Ben McAdams**

The right encouragement always seemed to find me when I needed it. Whenever I was at the end of myself and my strength, someone seemed to pop their head into my corner and offer some of their strength so I could keep going.

The emails, texts, videos, letters, DMs, and conversations carried me when I had nothing left to offer, because what we say to people matters. Our words have the terrible potential to tear down, but they also have immense power to build up.

35

Trial (Day Two)

November 13, 2019

On day two, I went through the same routine.

I woke up early, put on my second of four new shirts, drove to Chabad, and then headed downtown. After a quick stop at the D.A.'s office, we walked through the alleyway and went straight to the courthouse.

This time we used the back door.

My sentiment for using the main entrance was already gone. I was locked in and focused. No time for fun—it was time to tell my story. Donna and I had gotten through all the basics on day one—I was eight, we were homeschooled, and I knew not to touch women.

Today we were getting to the heavy stuff.

Right before we got into the abuse, Donna introduced Exhibit #2 to the court.

During one session with Dr. Michaels, he gave me a piece of advice. He told me to go to my parents' house and find a picture of myself at eight years old to remember why I was doing this.

That's exactly what I did.

I'd been carrying that picture around in my pocket to every hearing ever since.

That's who I was fighting for.

Weeks earlier, I showed the picture to Donna, and she realized that although it may be difficult to look at a six-foot twenty-eight-year-old wearing a nice suit and think of him as a victim, the real victim was the eight-year-old in the picture. We blew it up and presented it to the court.

"Do you know who this is?" she asked.

"That's a picture of me."

"And how old were you in this photo?"

"Around eight or nine."

The jury shifted nervously, and off we went. I told them everything.

Episode one.

Episode two.

Episode three.

Meanwhile, the unnamed man was back in the courtroom. Whenever I looked over, he was staring at me. Smirking. Smiling. Rolling his eyes.

Episode four.

Episode five.

Episode six.

Episode seven.

"In your estimation, how many times did this happen?"

"Dozens," I said.

Donna paused for what felt like an eternity to let that reality sink in as the jury stared at the picture. Then she continued asking questions about why I let the episodes continue.

"I thought this was our screw-up," I said as I began to explain how twisted up I was in a web of shame.

Right then, Judge Trease chimed in, "Ms. Kelly, Counsel, we are going to take a five-minute break."

Did I just say "screw-up" from the stand? Oh no, why did I say that? She's going to kick me off.

But those two words were the least of Judge Trease's worries. She had her eyes on someone else—the unnamed man.

"Counsel, there's an individual in the courtroom who will be barred from the courtroom for the rest of the trial. That's the gentleman in the back with the glasses." She went on to talk about the smirks and gestures she'd seen.

While she was speaking, the man got up to leave, but Judge Trease stopped him in his tracks. "Stay here," she said. "I'm not done. I warned him at the beginning of the trial that certain conduct is not appropriate."

And she didn't stop there. While he stood in front of the entire courtroom listening, she kept going.

Then he was removed and forbidden from coming back in.

That's what day two was like. It wasn't a civil get-together. It was open hostility.

———

The intensity continued to build, but it reached a boiling point when Donna introduced Exhibit #3—a recorded phone call between the witness and the defendant.

Every juror did a double take.

Remember, for the last day and a half, Vina had two interpreters sitting on either side of her. Months earlier, Joshua had said she didn't understand English. Up until this point, the jury had never heard Vina speak.

For all they knew, she couldn't understand the English language— that was about to change.

Donna hit play, and the entire courtroom heard Detective Blue's voice.

"Today's date is March 27, 2018. It's approximately 1110 hours. Detective Blue, Salt Lake City Police. We're going to be trying to call Vina at . . ."

Ring . . .

Ring . . .

"Hello?"

"Hi. Vina?"

"Hello!"

There was not a window in W49, but I was certain that outside, every drop of sunlight in the world burst through the clouds as the world was seen in a completely new light.

Reality dawned on the jury. The woman sitting before them, with headphones on and a taxpayer-funded translator sitting beside her, was speaking fluently. It was loud, and it was coming from every inch of the courtroom.

It was a lie.

The jury was being lied to.

There was a liar in their midst.

In the midst of all hell breaking loose, defense counsel realized that the time had come to object. Donna was objecting to his objection. The judge was trying to rule on the objection, but counsel couldn't hear her. Donna is great at many things, but technology isn't one of them. She was trying to figure out how to pause the recording but wasn't having any luck. The beautifully loud recording of Vina's English flowed throughout the courtroom.

Meanwhile, the translator was trying to translate Vina's own English words into Tongan for her—the irony was priceless.

I wanted to cry.

I wanted to dance.

I wanted to spike an imaginary football in an imaginary end zone and roar "Let's Go!" in front of 85,000 imaginary people. But witnesses aren't allowed to show emotion, so instead, I whispered a silent thank-you to God in the form of my second blessing. Then I stole a peek at the jury. All of them were focused in one direction, on one being. There was no sadness. There was no uncertainty. There was searing disappointment and blatant disapproval.

Eighteen eyes glared at Vina as if to say, "You've been lying to us for two days, and you show precisely zero remorse. What else should we assume you're lying about?"

It took me right back to that hard-backed chair at the Public Safety Building, Detective Blue scribbling talking points as I kept Vina on the line. It took all my composure to keep from shouting to the court the same question I asked Detective Blue all those months ago.

"Now do you believe me?"

———

We took a ten-minute break, and I bolted out of the courtroom.

I needed space. I needed to breathe. I probably needed to scream and let out some emotion, but that option was off the table, so instead I stood next to the bird statue and stared out the window.

Donna was done asking me questions, and it was time for the cross-examination, but Judge Trease decided we should take our lunch break and start the cross after lunch.

The interpreters had stepped out and gone to lunch early.

"All counsel is present," Judge Trease said on the record. "The defendant is present. She does not have a Tongan interpreter, but having listened to the telephone conversation, what I have to say, I think she'll understand."

The courtroom isn't typically a place for laughter, but I let out a little smirk.

———

Cross-examination was the most intimidating part of the week.

Even before walking back in from lunch, a sinking feeling in my stomach told me it was going to be Charlie to cross. This wasn't about substance; this was an attempt to cut down, destroy, and harm, and that is all Charlie knew how to do.

He didn't hold back.

"So these allegations were first reported to the police on January 30, 2018," Charlie asked as he paced around the room. "That's accurate, isn't it?"

"Yes."

"Now, have you ever heard of the MeToo Movement?"

"I have."

"The story you've told has been covered internationally, right?" he asked me.

"Yes."

"Do you enjoy being a MeToo celebrity?" he asked smugly.

"Could you define that question?"

"Well, haven't you made the statement that you are receiving a thousand calls a day? And you've flown to New York to do podcasts?"

"In the seventy-two hours after the story was published, I got about a thousand calls, but not anymore. And I was flying to New York anyway; I just happened to also get to record a podcast with a friend."

"And in the course of that podcast, didn't you say, 'God bless social media,' because your story had found its way to every corner of the globe?"

"Within the Jewish community, yes."

"So all of this has been very intentional?"

It felt endless. Charlie fired away with question after question about my intentions, accusing me of chasing clout while simultaneously asking me about all the uncomfortable details of the encounters.

"You were eighteen years old in 2009, correct?" he asked at one point.

"Yes."

"And Alavina Florreich was sixty years old, correct?"

"Yes."

"And so it's your testimony that this sixty-year-old lady, for some reason, wanted to engage with you sexually when you came home from school?"

"Yes."

"And do you have any knowledge as to whether or not she'd ever done something like that before?"

"Objection," Donna piped in at that point. "No foundation for that."

"Come on up," Judge Trease responded, so Donna and Charlie approached her bench to discuss whether or not Charlie should be allowed to ask me that. Meanwhile, I just sat on the stand helplessly and uncomfortably in front of a room full of reporters, a jury, and my poor family.

How did my life get to this point?

The cross-examination lasted two and half hours and went nowhere. The questions were all over the place and didn't seem to have any point. If I felt like he was heading in one direction, he'd suddenly stop his line of questioning and head in a different one.

If unpredictable was what he was going for, he at least accomplished that.

For me, the crowning moment came at the very end of the nearly three hours from hell.

In the initial police report, I told Detective Blue about how when I was away at school, I would count how many days it had been since my last encounter with Vina—like an addict counting days of sobriety.

Charlie took that line and tried to turn it on its head.

"Isn't it true that you would count how many days you would be sober, and by sober, you meant how many days until you could ejaculate again?"

What? How did you get that?

"I would count how many days since I had last ejaculated," I explained. The discomfort of having this conversation in such a public forum was nothing compared to my anger toward him for what he was trying to do.

"Okay," he said. "So you're away at school, thinking this is an addiction, so you count down the days to the end so you could come home and cum on Alavina?"

You've got to be kidding me.

Fight for yourself, one breath at a time.

"Like any addiction," I responded as calmly as I could, "I didn't want it to happen. That's why I would count the days of sobriety as a good thing. Not looking forward to coming home."

Charlie narrowed in on my words, like a predator thinking he had his prey trapped.

"Then why didn't you tell anyone?" he asked, a smug smile on his face.

I had been given one important rule by Donna before trial. Don't rehearse your answers. Let them come honestly and naturally to you. I made one exception. At some point during trial, this million-dollar question was going to hang in the air. Why did it take twenty years to report? I had thought quite a bit about how to best articulate the answer to that. I hadn't expected the opportunity to land that punch to present itself in such magnificent fashion. Charlie stuck out his jaw, and I led with a closed fist.

"Because of exactly what's happening right now."

That was the prick in the giant balloon; the tension began to ooze out of the room.

"Being cross-examined?"

"Because I'm being called a liar and an aggressor."

Dropping that line felt really good. And throwing Charlie off his guard was validating. For years, I was afraid of talking about everything that happened because most people wouldn't believe me. Most people have the same reaction the prospective jury members had when they heard about a sexual abuse case with a male victim. Surely it doesn't work like that, right? It can't.

That narrative is entrenched so deep in our culture that I shoved aside my eight-year-old self for years. *Sorry, buddy. We can't tell anyone about all that. No one will believe us.*

Charlie had strolled into his own trap, and he was caught in his words. "No further questions," he said a few short minutes later.

From there, I had a short redirect with Donna and then an even shorter recross examination, and that was it.

I was excused.

———

"Your Honor, the people call Detective Kevin Blue to the stand."

By this point, it was 3 p.m., and I had been on the stand all day. I was more than happy to step aside and let someone else be the center of attention, and Detective Blue did not disappoint. He didn't walk to the stand; he strutted. He strutted like Aaron Judge going up to the plate in front of a packed-out Yankee Stadium while his walk-up song blasted through the speakers.

There was a chair on the witness stand, and it faced straight out toward the courtroom. He walked right up and turned it directly toward the jury, leaning back and looking each one of them in the eyes.

We both knew this was over.

Within fifteen minutes, they were playing the video footage from the day they brought Vina in for questioning, the day following the pretextual phone call. During the video, she openly admitted how sorry she was for touching me.

Donna would share repeatedly with our team what a masterful job Detective Blue had done in the interview. Toward the end, Vina had tried to explain away a lot of what had happened as "teaching a child and helping him with his curiosity."

"Would you do the same to your own grandchild?" he had asked patiently.

"No, that's gross!" she said, as she recoiled in horror.

"What about my kid? What if I asked you to watch my son, would you touch him to teach him and help him with his curiosity?"

"No!" Vina protested adamantly. "Not in that sexy way!"

For someone who was trying to present the argument that there had been no sexual intent to anything she had done, she hadn't done herself a whole lot of favors in that interview.

The courtroom was a mess. When I glanced over, real tears were coming from the jury, outdone only by the hung heads and slouched shoulders on the defense side of the courtroom. One of Vina's sons, who had done prison time himself and undoubtedly had a sense of what awaited her on the inside, was weeping openly.

Donna brought up the bodycam footage from the drive home next, and defense counsel tried to stomp that out. They argued that the footage was inadmissible in court because when they got back in the police car, they had not Mirandized her again.

Which is a fancy way of saying they hadn't read her rights.

Judge Trease sent the jury home and spent the rest of the day sorting through the motion. Ultimately, she decided the footage was admissible and would be played tomorrow morning.

Day two came to a close.

———

That night, we had a party in the conference room.

The tide had shifted drastically.

All the momentum was ours.

Twenty-four hours before, I had told Donna that I found her opening statement underwhelming and the defense counsel to be much more intimidating.

As we celebrated that night, I laughed at the thought. There wasn't a single jury member driving home thinking about the opening statements. Those were a thing of the past.

Donna's slow start was on purpose.

Another chess move from a master.

36

Trial (Day Three)

November 14, 2019

"Judge Trease just told us she does not know how this case ended up in trial."

That was the news I started day three of trial with. Donna and I were sitting in the closet outside the courtroom after she returned from meeting with Joshua, Charlie, and a very animated Judge Trease, who wanted the attorneys to return to their parties and figure out a settlement.

"Is there a settlement you are willing to take?" she asked.

"Yes," I responded confidently, "as a matter of fact, there is—one first-degree felony."

After everything Charlie put me through the day before, I felt a little less merciful than I had in the months leading up to trial; I wasn't going to go to sentencing and ask for a lenient sentence. But if Vina were willing to admit to one first-degree felony, I'd be satisfied.

That was that. Donna didn't need to hear any more. Our conversation only lasted a couple of minutes. But by the time we got back into the courtroom, defense counsel was already back inside. Their conversation was even quicker.

When the attorneys had walked out of Judge Trease's chambers, she told both sides to consider seven second-degree felonies as a starting point for negotiations.

That was never going to fly for us. Apparently it wasn't an option for them either. They weren't even willing to consider it. Even though Judge Trease had already said she had no idea how this case ended up in trial, they decided they felt confident enough to roll the dice and take their chance with the jury.

That's how polarizing the room was. Judge Trease drew a circle between us, a possible compromise, and neither party was even remotely interested.

"Tense" isn't the right word to describe the feeling in the air.

Just get through this and it will all be over.

That became my mantra for day three. This was a test of wills, and as long as I could muster the patience and perseverance to wait them out, it would all go away.

Vina didn't even have the headphones over her ears at this point. The interpreters continued talking into the microphones; there just wasn't anyone listening on the other side. The inauthenticity reverberated through the room with every Tongan word.

The third day of trial started with the bodycam footage—good news for us and bad news for them. In the footage, Vina talked about how nice our family was and admitted how sorry she was for touching me, completely contradicting the tale the defense had tried to spin for the last two days. The inauthenticity, once again, reverberated through the room.

The defense counsel's last hope was their cross-examination of Detective Blue, so Charlie got up and did his worst.

It got nasty.

Vulgar.

Inappropriate.

Condemning.

At one point, Charlie referred to me as a rapist. At another, he asked Detective Blue if he was familiar with the case of Jussie Smollett, a man who got caught staging a hate crime and ended up in prison.

"Objection, Your Honor," Donna cried out from her table, more heated and flustered than I've ever seen her.

"Sustained!" responded a visibly annoyed Judge Trease.

Charlie smirked, the insinuation already clearly laid out before the jury.

It seemed that scorched earth was the only real play Charlie had left.

He tried every angle he could think of to get us to admit we were making this whole thing up to get attention. Meanwhile, the picture of my eight-year-old self sat quietly in my pocket, all his greatest insecurities about coming forward playing out in front of him.

Detective Blue wasn't fazed in the slightest. With confidence and calmness, he outlasted Charlie's charade and was dismissed.

He was our last witness.

With that, our case came to a close, and it was time for the defense counsel's turn. They would need to pull out all the stops to try to muster a come-from-behind win.

That's not what happened.

———

They called their first witness, a former employer of Vina, the mother of perhaps the only household Vina spent more time nannying at than ours. They knew her. They loved her. And so she agreed to get up on the witness stand.

Initially, Donna wasn't planning to cross-examine any of their witnesses. After all, this trial was not a referendum on Vina as a human being. The trial was to figure out if the incidents actually happened. Dignifying their pointless testimony wasn't worth it by her count.

"Would you say the defendant is honest and trustworthy?" Joshua asked.

"Absolutely, I think she's very trustworthy," the mother said confidently.

Sitting right behind Donna, I saw her ears perk up like a dog picking up a scent. Remember, since this woman was a witness, she wasn't allowed in the courtroom for the first half of trial.

She didn't get to see what everyone saw.

She didn't hear the phone call.

She didn't see the bodycam footage.

"You indicated you heard about this case on the news," Joshua continued. "After hearing about it, did you as a parent have any concern for your children?"

"I did not."

"Did you speak with your children about this event?"

"I did," she assured the court.

"After that conversation, did you gain any or have any concerns about your children?"

"I did not."

"No further questions," Joshua said, satisfied.

Then Donna broke her own rule and got up to cross. "You testified that you believe Mrs. Florreich to be an honest and trustworthy person, right?" Donna started.

"Yes."

"Would it change your opinion to know that she admitted to the police that she touched a young boy's penis to teach him about sex?" Donna asked.

"Um," the mother responded, flustered. "Would it change my opinion?"

"Yes, would you still consider her trustworthy with your children?"

Silence.

"I'm sorry. Can you explain your question?" she asked, trying to delay the inevitable.

A wise man once said, "The truth speaks in a loud voice." Whenever Charlie was asked to repeat one of his ludicrous questions during trial, he would unfailingly yell it even louder, as if the added decibels gave it the credibility it lacked. Donna needed no such thing. She kept her voice level and tried again.

"Would it change your opinion about her trustworthiness with your children?"

The witness was stuck and said the only thing someone who swore an oath to tell the truth could do. "I would say, yes."

That moment summed up the defense counsel's entire case. Vina was loved in our town. A long list of people trusted her and would be willing to jump up on a witness stand for her.

But none of those people had seen the bodycam footage.

None of them had heard the phone call.

None of them knew the truth.

Because who would ever believe the eight-year-old boy?

She ran out crying as soon as she got off the stand. We were excused for lunch, and I walked by her and her family. They were hugging, crying, and trying to soothe her. I walked by, and they stared at me like I was the worst person in the world.

Well, that pretty much sums up all of this, doesn't it?

Let me guess, I'm the bad guy here, right?

Somehow you are the victim in all this, aren't you?

How dare I get molested when I was eight and put you all through this?

The culmination of all those thoughts manifested in the look I shot across the hallway as I walked by. It was a dirty look, inspired by years of pain mixed with the fear I'd be misunderstood.

It set off a fountain of tears.

———

Bed, synagogue, court, bed, repeat.

That had been my routine all week. I hadn't had an ounce of physical exercise and next to no fresh air in days.

Team Avremi headed back to the D.A.'s office for lunch, but instead, I headed out for a walk.

Downtown was about as busy as you'd expect on a Thursday afternoon. I walked down the street fuming. Feeling mad, sad, and misunderstood all at the same time.

There was one place that wasn't busy at all—Bar X.

You know what? I need a drink.

The bar was empty, which is expected at 12:30 on a weekday. I walked in, dressed to the nines, sat down by myself, and ordered a beer.

Just get through this and it will all be over.

By the time I finished my first drink, I still had plenty of time, so I asked the waitress for one more.

"Well, we have a policy here . . ." she said.

Oh, here we go again. Another policy. The one place I thought I could go to get away from rules and regulations.

"What's the policy?" I asked as politely as I could muster.

"If you order more than one drink before 1 p.m., you gotta tell us what's going on."

"Tell you what," I said, with a grin that felt good to spread across my face, "pour me a second beer and pull up a chair."

We had a good laugh. She went and grabbed me another beer and then sat down and listened. We talked for about five minutes until I figured I should probably let her get back to work.

Those five minutes helped me immensely.

It may sound like a small thing, and at some level, it was. But for me, in the middle of day three of trial, it made all the difference.

That's the thing about humans. We have the propensity to cause so much pain in each other's lives. We hurt each other, abuse each other, lie to each other, blame each other, and call each other all sorts of awful names.

But we also have the propensity to help.

Our actions can hurt, but they can also heal.

Bar X was not the place I was expecting to meet the friend I needed at that moment.

I've learned over the years, that's usually how it works.

_____

Just get through this and it will all be over.

I kept repeating my mantra as I walked back to the courtroom for what was shaping up to be a long afternoon of defense witnesses.

Donna was waiting for me outside.

There was a development over lunch. Judge Trease had called both parties in to discuss the afternoon. She explained that she didn't want to spend the rest of the day debating Vina's character. If the defense had a witness who could testify why any of the seven accounts were untrue, fine. But she was putting her foot down against any more character witnesses.

The defense counsel didn't have anything to say in response.

That was it.

Donna presented her case over seventy-two hours.

The defense's case lasted all of fifteen minutes.

No evidence. No ace of spades. Just one witness who ran out crying.

_____

With the defense counsel formally resting their case, there was a wrinkle we were going to hit sooner than anticipated.

When the defense rests, before both sides move on to jury instructions and closing arguments, the defense traditionally makes a Motion for Directed Verdict, effectively asking the judge to dismiss the case on their own, without ever sending it to the jury.

All the rookies on my side sat up straight in their seats when they heard that from Joshua's mouth.

I chuckled.

Motions for Directed Verdict were the epitome of a Hail Mary.

Why is it so normal for me to know that?

Why couldn't I be a novice like everyone else?

Why was my life this way?

The Hail Mary didn't work. The defense counsel chucked the ball into the air, sending it soaring toward the end zone. But just as the crowd stood up on their feet, watching in slow motion, the ball hit the turf thirty yards short of the end zone, rolled around for a bit, and came to a stop.

The Motion for Directed Verdict was denied.

———

During court, you spend the entire day trying to ignore your emotions. There's no space to process them in the middle of the battle without risking losing your edge. It's not safe.

Instead, you push them down and build a dam to keep them there.

When we were excused at the end of day three, I got into my car, and before I could even put the key in the ignition, the dam broke. I took off my hat, loosened my tie, and tried to find my breath as all the pain, anger, frustration, and confusion spilled out.

Did Charlie really call me a liar and a rapist?

Jussie Smollett? Really?

I could see all the people giving me death stares all day. As if I was the one in the wrong.

I was the one who was sexually abused at eight years old.

What am I missing here?

It all came bubbling up to the surface. Thank God tomorrow was Friday. This was all going to end, and it couldn't come soon enough.

37

Trial (Day Four)

November 15, 2019

I walked up to the courthouse on Friday morning feeling like Kerri Strug.

At the 1996 Olympics, the USA Gymnastics team was in contention for a gold medal. Kerri Strug was the final competitor; she had a chance to seal the victory for her country. But during her first vault routine, she came down wrong and tore two ligaments in her left ankle. Unfortunately, she still had another round, and the team wasn't allowed to bring in a substitute.

Her only option was to play through the pain.

She took a deep breath, ran full-bore down the vault runway, and in one of the greatest moments in Olympic history, landed her second vault on one ankle. She stuck it, saluted the judges while hopping on her right leg, secured the gold medal, and then collapsed to the floor.

There is a famous picture of a trainer carrying her off as she waved to the crowd—the trainer's name is Larry Nassar.

Kerri Strug persevered through all the pain. She was down an ankle, so she competed with one. That's how I felt. I was a shell of myself, running on empty physically, emotionally, mentally, and every other "ally" you can think of.

There's a price you pay when you go for several days with next to no sleep, food, or rest.

One more vault.

We just needed to get through the closing statements, and then it was out of our hands and into the jurors'.

Donna told me she had a rule for closing statements: no objections. Unless the defense counsel said something really, really bad, she never interrupted closing statements.

How bad could this be?

———

On my way back down the hallway, I saw the last face I was expecting to see. Charlie's friend was back. The one who apparently was there to wreak havoc.

When we locked eyes, the hatred was visceral.

I said a few choice words to him, and he returned the favor.

"Hey, Donna," I said very loudly, clearly addressing everyone as I turned the corner and entered the courtroom. "Isn't this the guy who isn't allowed to be in the building?" Charlie sprinted out into the hallway and started yelling at his friend, urging him to get out.

Donna was up first.

She got up and gave her closing argument, and it was good—really good. She fell back on everything that had been said over the last few days, and you could feel the jury molding around her, hanging on to each word.

When Charlie got up, the wheels came off.

"Ms. Kelly asked our witness, 'Well, if you found out these things would you still consider her honest and truthful?' I mean, if you found out she was Hitler," he said at one point, "would you still consider her trustworthy?"

Hitler?

That's your only plausible example of someone that's not honest and truthful?

Did you really just say Hitler?

It can't be.

You see the room you are in, right?

Do you see the Kippah I'm wearing? The ones my people wore on the way to the gas chambers? I'm right here. And my father's right behind me. Do you see him? Did you know his mom was sent to a work camp as a little girl because of the man you enjoy name-dropping? After informing me that she never objects to closing statements, Donna objected twice.

Not once—twice.

It was that bad.

Charlie finished his last thought, and I decided I would be okay if I never heard him say another word.

In this trial, the burden of proof was on Donna, so she got to go up one more time and have the last say. Her rebuttal was about twenty minutes long. She started it by playing the "not in that sexy way" recording. She paced around the floor, repeating that statement, making sure every member of the jury was clear that Vina's intent toward me was sexual.

Then Donna finished at the board.

"This is count one."

"This is count two."

"This is count three."

"This is count four."

"This is count five."

"This is count six."

"This is count seven."

"And I urge you to go in there and return with a guilty verdict. Guilty as charged on all seven counts."

I wanted to stand and clap, but you can't do that in court, so instead I sat and smiled.

The trial was over.

Up until that point, Judge Trease told the jury the same thing every time she had dismissed them: "Don't talk about it." But just past 11 a.m., after Donna's closing remarks, that changed.

"Members of the jury, you now have been given all the evidence and instructions in this case. The case is now submitted to you for your deliberation and determination of your verdict."

We headed out to the D.A.'s office and had lunch together.

At this point, Detective Blue was a part of the family, so we'd make lunch for him too, and he'd sit down and hang out.

"This will take some time. Ninety minutes is the absolute minimum," Donna explained during lunch. "Trust me. They get lunch on the state's dime. They don't want to pass that up. Just ordering it and eating it takes an hour at least. But I've seen this process take several hours."

After I finished lunch, I needed some fresh air.

I'd barely been outside all week, so while the rest of my team waited inside, I ventured out front and—for the first time in a very long time—attempted to experience life like a normal person.

Standing outside the D.A.'s office, my face basked in the glow of the cool sunlight of a beautiful Salt Lake City morning.

38

An "Admonition" She Called It

November 15, 2019
1:15 p.m.

An "admonition," she called it.

"There should be no outward reaction when the verdict is read," Judge Trease told us.

No matter what the verdict said, it would be emotional for both sides, and Trease didn't want to make the jury uncomfortable.

That would be the final reminder of how unrealistic and dramatized *Law & Order* is. No dramatic music, no gasps, no tears. In the real world, the moment is supposed to be strictly business.

Looking back, of all the truly laughable moments of trial, that one was up there. One of two things was about to happen: either a woman was about to be sentenced to prison for the rest of her life, or the jury was about to call someone who talked about a decade of childhood abuse a bald-faced liar.

Either way, we were supposed to keep quiet.

Okay, Judge Trease—we'll see.

All week I insisted on facing forward, even through the hardest parts of trial. But I couldn't do it. I couldn't bring myself to look up. To try to peer at the faces of the jurors and hope for some indication of which way they were leaning.

My neck was frozen at a slight tilt, facing down at my hands.

At the picture that had been in my pocket for a year and a half, for every day in court.

Exhibit #2.

So prominently displayed beside me during my testimony, now clenched in my hands. It was little Avremi alone that I had eyes for. Every bit of pain and heartbreak and aggravation I had undergone in this process, I'd sign up for it again and again if it meant finding closure for him. If it meant making things right by him. If it meant taking away one sliver of everything I had dumped on him for twenty years, I'd do it again.

I locked eyes with him and saw the sweetness of his innocence gazing back. An innocence I could never give back to him. An innocence that no verdict would replace or repair. An innocence gone forever, leaving him feeling that no one would ever stand in his corner again.

Not anymore.

Never again.

I had been there for him throughout this entire process and would be again, every single day forever more. The thought unified two deep pieces of me, and I immediately started to sob.

Judge Trease's warning ran through the back of my head in protest, but I couldn't stop the tears from flowing.

Months and years of tension overtook me.

Juror number 15 was the foreman. The verdict forms were handed to Judge Trease, and the clerk began to read the verdict into the record.

"State of Utah vs. Alavina Florreich, case number 181903863, we the jury find as follows. As to the first count, sexual abuse of a child, we find the defendant guilty. We further find that an aggravating factor has been proven."

Guilty.

The word that has changed so many lives for the better and worse. The word that provides some semblance of justice in an unjust world.

"As to the second count, sexual abuse of a child—guilty."

I stared down at the picture in my hand.

Do you hear it? The judicial system is letting you know they hear you. They believe you.

I was crying so intensely I could barely make out the words from the clerk, yet they almost seemed irrelevant. Rational thoughts began to form somewhere between the fifth and sixth guilty counts.

I am crying so loud I can't hear the verdict. I am seriously going to get thrown out of here.

I caught my breath long enough to hear the cherry on top, counts six and seven—guilty and guilty.

A clean sweep.

Seven for seven.

Eight complete strangers took no issue calling out what they knew to be true and false. The jury was gone long before I could compose myself to look back up—I never saw them again.

Slowly, the world came back into focus. Amy had been sitting next to me during the verdict, resourceful as ever with a wad of tissues whenever I was ready for them. I looked down the row and saw my mother and Sheina holding hands so tightly that their knuckles were white as plaster. Behind me, Gillian was wiping tears from her eyes.

My breathing was returning to normal, yet my chair was still shaking. That's when I realized my father was crying so violently that he was slumped over onto my chair, rocking it back and forth.

I stole a peek across the aisle.

Not a visible emotion to be seen.

Absolute incredulity.

Some puzzled looks up at the judge.

Denial through and through.

The lawyers were back to lawyering. Something about dates, sentencing reports, and motions. "At some point, we're going to need to discuss the issue of her custody status," said Judge Trease.

"Yes, Your Honor," Joshua said, jumping from his chair. He proceeded to rattle off a laundry list of reasons why his client was the ideal and model defendant and why she should be allowed to stay home until sentencing.

Ever the cool voice of reason, Donna rose to speak. "Your Honor, I'd remind the Court that there has been a material change in the circumstances of the case. With the defendant now being found guilty of seven felonies, five of them bringing a mandatory prison sentence, the incentive to flee increases tremendously."

Judge Trease asked if both parties had said their piece and indicated she'd think about it—I figured we were headed for another court recess.

She thought about it for approximately one and a half seconds.

"With a guilty verdict on the record, I am revoking the defendant's bail and ordering her to be taken into custody, pending her sentencing on the date to be determined by the Court."

For several months, Judge Trease had one mantra, "innocent until proven guilty." Not anymore. All that changed with the verdict—the jury had spoken. She had been proven guilty.

Twenty months since the first time she first got arrested.

Twenty-two months since I first made the phone call.

This was over.

Almost instantly, as though her words had flipped an unseen switch, one of the bailiffs stepped out of the aisle and over to the defense table. He firmly placed his arm on Vina's right shoulder and ordered her to stand.

The all-too-familiar sound of handcuffs closing rang out through the courtroom, and my abuser was formally taken into custody. But this time, there was no bail to look forward to after a night at County.

This was custody that she would spend a very, very long time in. Lies, threats, and slander had risen and fallen. The state's repeated offers to plead guilty to just one count faded into oblivion like a dismissed dream.

Vina was in cuffs.

I allowed myself one fleeting moment of internal victory and visibly nodded my head as she sat back down between her attorneys, her arms uncomfortably behind her back.

I couldn't get out of the courtroom quickly enough. As soon as the last minutiae had been wrapped up and court was in recess for the last time that week, I made a beeline for the doors. Emotion was bubbling up again, the highs and lows all crashing together to form one tidal wave that threatened to engulf me. I was yearning for the quiet of the hallway once again.

Pop. Pop. Flash. Pop. Pop.

Cameras were right up in my business, recording every moment. For all I knew about healthy vulnerability, I had always made an effort to appear composed in front of a camera—call it one last unhealthy insecurity.

Every one of my insecurities had fallen by the wayside over trial; this one was no exception. My emotions needed release, and they were going to find it, one way or another.

I got to my bird statues, looked out over Main Street, and lost it.

————

It was almost fitting that Detective Blue was the first one to come over. He wasn't a cop anymore. He was in it with us, and I cried on his shoulder for a good minute.

My father was next, embracing me with more emotional vulnerability than I'd ever seen from him.

"Vina will never hurt you again," my mother reminded me as she handed me a bottle of water—I took a sip and drew in enough breath to make the walk back down the hallway.

Hugs and high-fives abounded as I walked. Cameras were everywhere.

> *Blessed are you, Lord our God, King of the Universe, who*
> *has enabled us to reach this occasion, who has kept us to*
> *this day.*

I made my fourth and final blessing—marking the moment as I walked back down the hallway toward the exit.

————

The reality was sinking in. The inescapable truth that Vina was never getting out. But I wasn't whooping and hollering. I wasn't lighting up a cigar. Nothing in me wanted to pop champagne.

Instead, I went and picked up my kids from preschool.

"How'd it go?" the director of the school asked.

"It went well," I told her.

Which was true. It did go well, but I didn't feel any better.

The sun set on the longest week of my life, and Shabbat finally began. As Sheina lit the Shabbat candles, I realized Vina was having slop for dinner.

Is she holding on to the denial?

Would that ever start to fade?

Was any of this worth it?

Questions I had only just begun to wrestle with. It was done. We did it. But what did we accomplish?

There are only two words I've ever really wanted to hear from her: "I'm sorry." I suppose, at some level, all of this was an attempt to get those words. I wanted Vina to own up to what she did, apologize for lying to me, and confess that she understood her actions didn't make me a better husband. They poisoned my mind and made every relationship in my life more complicated.

That's what I wanted.

Instead, I just got a lot of denial and dirty looks.

Because of that, she's going away forever. We won the trial, but it didn't feel like it. This could've been a win-win, but denial dragged it down into a lose-lose.

Gillian came for dinner that night with two friends. We made a lot of toasts, drank a lot of wine, and cried a lot of tears.

But it wasn't a party. That wouldn't be the right word.

It was heavy.

It was somber.

Judge Trease had given us an admonition, a warning not to celebrate, and hours later, I was still following her orders.

39

You're Human

December 19, 2019

I hadn't stepped foot in the Matheson Courthouse in over a month.

The trial was over, and after several sessions with Dr. Michaels and good conversations with trusted friends, I felt like I had processed the week. But the aftermath remained. I had sentencing looming in the back of my mind and was still getting a lot of attention (good and bad) from all the press. The *Deseret News* released a ten-minute video telling my story, and the response was overwhelming.

I was searching for some semblance of normal, a new normal, a post-trial normal. While I just wanted to be the local Rabbi, focusing on his community, I was also getting amazing opportunities to answer questions, help people process their abuse, and make it through the most challenging and confusing seasons of their lives.

By all accounts, December 19 was normal. It was everything I'd come to expect on a Thursday, until it wasn't. I got home from the synagogue early enough to put the kids to bed, but while we were going through their typical routine, my lungs suddenly felt like someone had them in one hand, squeezing them in a vice.

Am I having a heart attack?

My Apple Watch informed me that my heart rate was 185 beats per minute—information that was both helpful and horrifying. I made it over to my bed and sat down to catch my breath and gather my thoughts.

What's happening to me?

Eventually, the vice around my lungs began to loosen, so I walked over and finished putting the kids to bed, doing my best to pretend everything was fine.

But it happened again.

A second episode.

This time worse.

The tightness in my lungs had moved up to my chest, as if the Hulk was squeezing my heart in the palm of his hands. I glanced back down at my Apple Watch, but that made things worse—210.

I'm dying.

I need to tell Sheina I love her.

I thought that was the end. After everything I'd been through, I was going to be taken out by a heart attack in my own bedroom.

———

My time at Urgent Care didn't last long. They hooked me up to an EKG, but I had another episode right in the middle of it, and they immediately sent me to the hospital.

Thankfully the hospital was quiet; they were able to get me right in to see the doctor. After a fourth episode in the Emergency Room, the on-call cardiologist came back into my room.

"Hey there, Avrohom," he said. "I read your file, and I see what's happening. Can I ask you a question?"

"Yeah."

"Is it possible I've seen your picture in the news a lot recently?"

I smiled grimly and nodded my head.

"You are having a panic attack," the doctor said.

I wanted to cry.

Panic attacks? Really? I just went through the hardest season of my life, and the only thing I have to show for it is panic attacks?

I'm twenty-eight, a survivor of sexual abuse. And now, to add to my ever-growing Twitter bio, I suffer from panic attacks.

"Really?" I told the doctor. "I'm only twenty-eight years old."

He smiled and nodded in understanding. "Seventy-five percent of the population get panic attacks. Given everything you've been through over the past few weeks, I'm surprised it's taken you this long to come see me."

My heart had calmed down, and they were ready to release me, but the doctor sensed from my lack of a response that I wasn't super amused. Before I left, he came back into my room and handed me a pair of scissors.

"You're free to go, but first, I want you to cut off your bracelet," he said.

I cut it off and held it in my hands. Next, he handed me a marker.

"I want you to write two words on the back of the bracelet: 'You're Human.' If the panic attacks ever come back, remember, you're in good company with the rest of the world—three out of four adults go through the exact same thing."

You're human.

———

That bracelet will be in my wallet every day for the rest of my life, right next to Immanuel's picture of whatever it is he drew for me before my first day in trial.

Survivors of childhood sexual abuse have long been known as the loneliest creatures in the world. My newly acquired panic attacks could've become the next thing that isolated me. I could've let them convince me that I'm different and that no one will ever understand. I could've let them drag me back down into the shadows and suffer in silence.

Or I could remember I'm human.

It's human to be vulnerable.

It's human to want to cry.

It's human to be faced with challenges.

It's human to be scared.

It's human to panic.

Life is less about the things going on in your life and more about how you perceive them. Challenges, hardship, and pain don't make you an outcast or an outsider; they make you a human.

40

Sentencing

March 12, 2020

Traditionally, two things happen at sentencing.

The victim gets to read an impact statement, and the perpetrator apologizes and promises to change their ways in hopes of lowering their sentence.

Judge Trease only had one decision to make that day. At the end of sentencing, she would decide whether the sentences should run consecutively or concurrently.

The best-case scenario for Vina was for the sentences to run concurrently, which would mean that while she served her sentence for the first count, that time also went toward numbers two through seven.

The worst case for Vina was Judge Trease deciding she needed to serve her sentences consecutively, meaning once she served five years for the first count, time would begin for the second count. Then five years after that, she would start on the third account, and so on and so forth.

———

Before sentencing, a pre-sentencing officer gathers both sides of the story and puts together a report.

In *Know My Name*, Chanel Miller wrote about getting screwed over by her pre-sentencing report—what she said was manipulated and used against her. So when my pre-sentencing officer called, I was more than a little skeptical.

"I want to let you know that I don't trust you," I said to the pre-sentencing officer when she called. "It's nothing personal, but I don't trust the system."

"I get that," she said kindly. That's not what I expected. "I get the distrust. But so you know, I'm not a compromiser. This isn't arbitration. I'm not in between you guys; I'm here to hear both sides of the story."

"Okay," I said. "You want me to say my piece? Here goes: She should go to jail for a very long time. Do you know why? Because in her mind, she's convinced she hasn't done anything wrong. Meaning, when she gets out, there's nothing to say she won't do this again."

———

If you can believe it, sentencing got pushed off.

Again.

And again.

And again.

But at that point, I couldn't care less. Vina was in prison. For all I cared, we could wait for hell to freeze over before we got to the sentencing.

In January, Donna reached out to let me know the report was complete, and although she wasn't allowed to send it to me, I could drive down to the D.A.'s office and see it in person.

By this point, I was a frequent flyer at the D.A.'s office. Unlike my first visit, I felt very comfortable walking through the sliding doors.

When someone is in the D.A.'s office, there is a good chance their day isn't going great. There was another young man sitting in the lobby, no older than twenty-three. As he sat there, his legs shook so hard they rattled the several-hundred-pound bench.

I knew that leg shake.

I knew the inability to make eye contact, to return the "hey" nod from a stranger. I knew what it was like to pray for the ground to open up and swallow you before you head off to have the conversation you are inevitably there for.

I did what I wished someone could have done for me on my first visit; I leaned in a little closer and made eye contact.

"First time?" I asked him.

He gave me a hurried half-nod in response.

"Not to worry, bud," I said. "They take good care of you around here."

I'm not sure if he registered my warm wishes, but it felt like the shaking slowed.

———

"Well, Avremi," Donna said as I walked into her office, "I'll have you know the pre-sentencing report makes you look like a prophet."

Apparently Vina had a much different conversation with the pre-sentencing officer than I did. While sitting in prison, she told her she was shocked by the verdict and had no idea why the jury found her guilty. Ultimately, she told her she shouldn't be surprised because everyone knows I have friends on the jury.

Complete denial.

Zero admission of guilt.

Page two quoted me saying I didn't think she realized she was doing anything wrong. Then page three quoted Vina saying she hadn't done anything wrong.

"As I said," Donna repeated, "it makes you look like a prophet."

———

On my way home, I stopped for a few groceries.

I felt pretty good by that point because I realized there wasn't much left to do. I didn't need to accomplish much with my impact statement.

When I sat down to write it, I could spend most of the time addressing my experience, telling Vina and the defense counsel how I felt about everything that happened.

When I walked into the store, I ran into someone unexpected. The young man from the lobby of the D.A.'s office was right in the middle of the produce section, searching for some ripe bananas. He was wearing the same clothes as that morning, had the same overwhelmed look on his face, and was only slightly more composed as he put the fruit in his cart.

"Hope it all worked out?" I managed to croak as I walked by. This time I got a full nod, a valiant half-smile, and thankful eyes before he hurried off.

As small as that moment was, I'll never forget it.

Everyone shops for groceries. And when we do, we pass other people in the aisles doing the same thing. It's easy to see each person as an obstacle standing in your way, slowing you down from getting to the ketchup.

But every single one of those people has a story.

They may be in the middle of the most joyous day of their life, stopping to get a celebratory snack after winning the PowerBall, or they may be coming from the D.A.'s office on the heels of one of the most challenging days of their life.

I don't know why God allows bad things to happen. I don't understand where God was in the middle of my darkest moments. But I do know the pain we experience is not meaningless. It changes our perspective on life and the people we meet. It teaches us how to empathize with a broken world, how to see the person standing in the produce section as a human being who could use a friendly smile and an acknowledgment that someone sees them.

On some level, people are immensely complicated.

And yet, on another level, we are incredibly simple.

We just need to know we aren't alone; we need to know someone sees us, like Elizabeth Smart driving down the mountain to sit in the back of a courtroom and smile. Sometimes, just showing up is enough.

The night before sentencing, I put the kids to bed, grabbed a cold beer, and sat down to watch the Jazz game—doing my best to unplug and put my worries about the sentencing down.

I got to my couch just in time for tip-off, only to discover that the game had been pushed back five minutes. As the officials talked, five minutes turned to ten, and then they finally announced that the game was being postponed due to unforeseen events.

Everyone in the stadium was instructed to remain calm and exit the building. As a general rule of thumb, whenever a large crowd is instructed to stay calm, it's not a good situation.

Shortly after, it was confirmed that a Jazz player named Rudy Gobert tested positive for a new virus called COVID-19.

Sentencing was different than trial.

I felt much more comfortable letting my siblings and friends attend.

We all sat down as Judge Trease called the court to order, and for the first time, the side door opened. The courtrooms at the Matheson Courthouse all have a side door connected to a private hallway, which they use to transport prisoners. The clanking of chains filled the courtroom, reaching my ears before I had a good vantage point of Vina. Then she slowly made her way through the courtroom, wearing an orange jumpsuit.

Everyone was staring at me.

For several weeks, all my friends and family seemed very concerned about how I would respond when I saw the chains and the orange. I didn't give them anything to write home about. No smile, no tears, no semblance of any type of emotion. Instead, I just sat there stone-faced.

You did this.

This did not have to be this way.

I'm not going to react because I didn't do this. You did.

————

During the trial, Donna ran the show for our team. She was the one call-ing the shots and carrying the team. Sentencing was different. She got up and spoke for a few minutes, pointing out that, despite all the noise from the defendant, we were still missing those two magic words: *I'm sorry.*

"But that's not why we're here today," she continued. "I'd like to invite Mr. Zippel to the stand to read his statement."

Sharing my impact statement was a very emotional experience for me. I didn't pull any punches in my statement. I said what I wanted to say and am really proud of what I came up with.

The entire statement is in the back of this book.

In a perfect world, the day would've ended right after I read my state-ment, but the world is far from perfect. Vina got up and rambled on and on about all the same stuff they'd been trying to say.

She addressed my parents and thanked them for the opportunity to be with our family for so many years.

Cringe.

She thanked Charlie and Joshua for their dedicated service to her case, and for loving her "and her beautiful brown skin." The implication was clear: everyone who was not her attorney was racist.

Barf.

And then she addressed Sheina and me, reminding us once again that she thought the phone call was a joke. In her written statement to the judge, she had literally said, "I thought at first it was a big April Fool's joke played on me."

I'm so done with all this.

Rodger's speech was even worse. Somehow hearing him was more infuriating than listening to Vina. I couldn't figure out if it was denial or ignorance, but he was still grasping onto the narrative that his wife was innocent. Even after a phone call was played in open court, when Vina confessed it was her memories with me that allowed her to be with him, he still doubled down, continuing to live in his own world, constructed by his own lies.

A luxury I couldn't afford—those lies caused my world to crumble around me.

I can't listen to this anymore.

Joshua got the last word, and his speech was everything that is wrong with criminal defense. He talked about all the letters they'd received about how wonderful a woman Vina is.

At that point, I felt like I was going crazy. They were still trying to prove her character. Vina could be Mother Teresa every other moment of her life, but if she abused a child, she's guilty.

His final point destroyed me.

He talked about how different this trial would've been if it had happened twenty years ago. We'd all agree justice needed to be served back then, but time had passed. The notion that somehow the horror of the actions diminished over time and should count less because of elapsed time is the single most offensive thing you can say to a survivor.

Do you think I deal with it less because it was twenty years ago?

Whether the abuse happened two days, two months, two years, or two decades ago, the horror is the same. Any attempt to diminish the pain is offensive.

The defense ended their time making one more plea to let Vina carry out her sentencing under house arrest; this time, the angle was Rodger's health. Because it was always something or someone else for Vina. It was never about simply owning up to her mistakes.

If you want to go home to your sick husband, say sorry.

Judge Trease was way ahead of me. "In cases such as this, it's a requirement that the defendant admit the offenses and be accepted for sex offender treatment before they can be considered for any probation. That is not something that has been shown in this case."

Not something that has been shown in this case.

Her words sizzled like a fat steak on the fire. The decision was made; Vina would serve all five first-degree felonies consecutively.

What was it that warranted that decision? Was it my statement? Her statement? Rodger's statement?

No one knows. And no one ever will.

That was it. When Judge Trease dismissed us, there were hugs in the hallway—a feeling of finality. The reporter left our courtroom and ran off to the Capitol because the Governor was holding a press conference in which he was imposing the first round of COVID-19 measures.

Apparently the world around us was ending.

Meanwhile, Vina would enter the custody of the Utah State Prison at the ripe old age of seventy years and six months, and one would speculate that chances are slim she will ever leave.

41

Advocacy

2020-Present Day

During Rabbinical school, I had lots of different roommates. They were all randomly assigned, and some worked out better than others.

One of my favorite roommates I ever had was a guy named Gershon. Gershon was wicked smart, with a dry sense of humor that was the perfect complement to mine, topped off with a hysterical Mancunian accent. We are still good friends to this day.

I met Gershon the day we both moved into our dorm room. While unpacking our things and setting up our stuff for the year, Gershon took out what looked like a series of syringes and vials and started placing them in our fridge—not what I was expecting.

He was used to seeing those odd looks at this point in his life and figured he'd give me an explanation before I even asked. "I'm a diabetic," he explained. "This is insulin, to help me correct my blood sugar."

That was a new one for me. I had never met a person with diabetes before. In the months to come, I'd find out firsthand just how normal of a life Gershon lived. Besides keeping his insulin close by and watching his diet, his life was unaffected.

But on day one, I didn't know any of that, so I asked him a question we still laugh about today. "Hey, Gershon," I said with an anxiousness birthed from ignorance, "is diabetes contagious?"

He just stared and smiled. "Diabetes isn't, but stupidity is."

The line was the beginning of a great friendship.

Four months later, my brother Chaim was diagnosed with juvenile diabetes.

When the news came in, my parents had a terrible time with it. They were visibly upset, confused, and scared. My reaction was much different; I had familiarity. I was used to it; I had lived with a person with diabetes before, and I knew it would be okay, but without that familiarity, my parents were devastated.

When you know someone, it changes things.

Donna has a great line I've heard her use several times: "Everyone hates lawyers, aside for their cousin, who is a lawyer and a really good person." That's true, isn't it? People love to talk badly about lawyers, but they all have their friend's dad or an aunt, someone they know personally and trust.

It's occurred to me over the years that the same principle applies to survivors of sexual abuse. There is such a strong stigma surrounding survivors because a lot of people don't know one personally—or more accurately, most people don't know that they know one. When they meet a survivor, it changes the way they think about abuse. Stigmas thrive with distance, but proximity breaks them down.

My parents and I had fundamentally different responses to Chaim's diagnosis. They panicked while I stayed calm. The difference was that I knew Gershon, but they didn't.

After sentencing wrapped up and I was finally able to speak freely and openly about everything that had happened, I began to wonder if we could apply the same philosophy to advocacy.

I had an opportunity to participate in the SHINE Campaign, a non-profit organization that helps survivors of child abuse lead rich, fulfilling lives. The campaign's goal is to shine a light on survivors and show the world how possible it is to continue living life on the other side of abuse.

Teaming up with a former state senator and Deondra Brown, one of the foremost mentors I've been blessed to have in the advocacy space, we began to shine a light on our abuse, talking openly about both the pain it caused and the healing we've experienced since. All to break down the stigma and remind other survivors they aren't alone.

I'll never forget the first time I drove past one of the thirty-eight billboards our faces were plastered on. Those billboards were put up because every car could have a young survivor in it who aspires to be a musician, politician, or maybe even a Rabbi one day. We wanted them to know their abuse doesn't disqualify them. It's not a deal breaker; they can still pursue their dreams. I figured maybe I could be a Gershon for someone else—a reminder that when life hits us, we can decide to hit back harder.

Staring up at the billboard was a powerful moment, but I also had to laugh.

A few years ago, I wanted to keep my story a secret.

A few years ago, I told a police officer my name was Brian out of fear.

A few years ago, I had to pull over to the side of the highway and cringe when a news story with my initials was published.

Now there was a giant picture of my face on every highway in Utah highlighting my story—not what I expected.

———

Do you remember that Jazz game I told you about back in March of 2018? The one I went to with that friend from my community the day after recording the pretextual phone call with Vina? The one where I also dropped Chaim and Sarahle off at the arena right after telling them their nanny sexually abused me when I was a kid?

I never told you what happened during the game. I never told you about the special ceremony held between the third and fourth quarters that set the tone for much of my work as an advocate.

During the 2017-18 season, the Jazz uniforms had a jersey patch supporting Five for the Fight, an organization determined to stamp out cancer once and for all. Unbeknownst to me, of all the Jazz games that season, that specific night was Five for the Fight Night.

At the quarter break, they turned out every light in the building except for one lone spotlight that shone on center court, and the broadcast team asked everyone to take out their phones and keep them close to their chest so that the screen wasn't shining.

"If you are a survivor of cancer," the broadcaster said, "turn on the flashlight on your phone."

A couple hundred lights appeared throughout the arena, followed by a small smattering of applause.

The broadcaster continued. "If anyone has an immediate family member who was diagnosed with cancer, whether they survived or not, turn on your flashlight and shine your light to the world in honor of your loved one."

I had lost my Zaidy to brain cancer a few months before my wedding, so it was my honor to pull out my phone and shine my light into the world in his honor. A couple thousand other people joined me, and the once-dark arena began to glow.

"And now," the broadcaster said, setting up the finale, "anybody who knows anybody who has gone through this perilous battle with cancer, whether they lived to tell the tale or not, would you please turn on your light in their honor."

As you can imagine, every single phone turned on—18,306 lights brightened the arena as the place erupted in applause. The more powerful the clapping, the more daunting the realization. The broadcaster went on to explain the power of proximity. Cancer affects everyone, and if we want to end it, we all have a part to play—we are in this together.

I was less than thirty-six hours from having had to come to terms with the fact that child sexual abuse was an inescapable part of my life. And I was really learning a lot about the vulnerability that would become part and parcel of who I was moving forward. It was inspiring to be in that room, experiencing that sort of vulnerability and watching people openly talk about their proximity to an issue that still has some element of stigma around it.

I couldn't help but think that not everyone who was a cancer survivor actually turned on their phone in the first round of the exercise. But I'll tell you this: if they had asked the questions in reverse order, and the survivors saw the crowd, the community surrounding them, I think every one of them would've had their light on proudly.

There will always be a certain stigma and a certain discomfort that comes with attaching yourself to an issue with any sort of drama or tension around it. But when you realize, understand, and see how much it affects every single person, you feel compelled, you feel inspired, you feel empowered to lend your voice to that chorus of bravery.

I've always held on to that moment in my own battle.

My story is a flashlight in a dark arena—a light to remind any other survivor whose hands may be shaking as they consider whether or not they should hit that button and let the world know that they are not the only one. If they step out of the shadows, I can't promise they won't suffer, but I can promise they won't suffer alone.

———

Throughout my journey, there have been so many people who have taught me how to find my voice and say it how it is.

Just a few weeks after I told my story, back in 2019, there was another story being told in the local community. Joe Ingles, a fan favorite playing for the Jazz back then, came out and talked about the fact that his son Jacob had recently been given an autism diagnosis. Joe and his wife, Renae, decided to grab the bull by the horns, fully embrace the journey their family would be on, all in the hope of lightening the load for other families in similar tough spots.

Let's face it. When a child struggles with autism, we as a society expect the parents to mumble under their breath about their child's condition. Joe and Renae took the opposite approach. "NAH, WE'RE NOT GOING TO MUMBLE. OUR CHILD IS DEALING WITH AUTISM. THERE IS NOTHING TO BE EMBARRASSED ABOUT. MILLIONS OF KIDS GO THROUGH THE SAME THING EVERY DAY. YES, WE'RE YELLING. IN ALL CAPS."

Joe and Renae taught me and so many others around me a valuable lesson with their decision and with their incredible efforts in the years to come. Embrace who you are. Embrace your journey. Know what it is, understand what it is, and call it like it is.

No code words.

No wordplay.

No holding back.

Just speaking the truth.

Turning on that flashlight on your phone and holding it proudly to the sky.

Some people may still live in a space where survivors can't be Orthodox, or successful, or happy, or a productive part of this world. I know that space well. I lived in it for over a decade, but I don't live there anymore. I packed my bags and left.

If someone doesn't like it, if it makes them uncomfortable, then we will have to respectfully agree to disagree. I may not be what people expected, but that's because life was not what I expected. I had a whole lifetime ahead of me. I was going to be a Chabad Rabbi who made the world a better place like I had always wanted, and I was going to be normal, like everybody else—but God had a different plan.

One day I realized, if I wanted to make a difference in God's world, I should probably do it in the way God had in mind for me. I should probably trust God's plan for my life instead of trying to forge my own.

Since that day, I've been able to help person after person through some of the darkest and scariest moments of their lives. Every morning I wake up and realize I have the opportunity to tell my story. To take the evil I experienced and use it for good. To stand up for the people who are ashamed of their abuse and help them heal. To sit down with survivors who feel like they are on an island and show them they are not alone.

I'm an advocate.

I wasn't planning on being one, but it turns out that the most meaningful and rewarding version of my life was the one I was not expecting.

Impact Statement

*As read in the 3rd District Court,
Thursday, March 12, 2020*

Thank you, Your Honor.

Human beings can and often do spend a lifetime contemplating the impact of their own actions on the world around them, most of the time to no avail. What we do or don't do may seem largely significant or completely pointless to us in the moment, while we remain blissfully ignorant to the ripple effect it creates around us, whether intended or not. How much more so to try and describe the impact that someone else's actions may have had on us is surely an exercise in guesswork at best. Nonetheless, I appreciate the opportunity granted to me by the Court to do my best and attempt to share the effects of my abuser's actions on myself and those nearest and dearest to me.

If I may, I'd like to attempt and frame this conversation through the prism of several comments made at the trial. But first, a thought about the trial experience, and the impact that it has.

The statistics surrounding the secrecy about childhood sexual abuse are astounding. Suffice it to say that most survivors, whether male or female, don't want to talk about it to anyone, let alone press charges. Why is that? Because of the voices in their heads that stroke their fear and anxiety out of control. They won't believe me. They'll call me a liar. They'll mock me. They'll say I liked it; I asked for it even. They'll call me all sorts of disgusting names. On and on it goes. When someone works up the courage to find one token soul in this world, another human being that they feel safe with, to share their deepest and darkest secrets, we applaud them. Call them courageous. Remind them how brave they are. Inevitably, at some point, the conversation gets steered towards the possibility of involving law enforcement, and pursuing the path of the criminal justice system. At that point, the young person in question shares the fears mentioned above, certain that their decision to come forward will without a doubt actualize their anxieties! Nonsense, we tell them! No one would EVER say such things. We live in the United States of America, it's 2020, look how far we've come as a society. Those sorts of spiteful attitudes are a relic of the past, never to be returned to again. Okay, they say. I'll make the call.

Your Honor, after having been sexually abused for a decade, and making the decision to come forward about it, I was subjected to another form of abuse. This time, it didn't take place in the secrecy of a cramped basement bathroom, rather it took place in this courtroom, from this very podium. During the course of the trial, among a litany of hurtful, hateful and insensitive comments, I was referred to as "the rapist" by Charlie. Comparisons were made from my behavior to that of Jussie Smollett. During defense counsel's closing argument, Charlie wondered aloud why I wasn't being charged and prosecuted for forcible sodomy, only after he had performed a gesture miming masturbation in front of the jury. And in a courtroom, full of Jews who had lost members of their families to the atrocities of the Holocaust, reference was made by the defense counsel to Adolf Hitler. In the United States of America. In 2019.

As obscene and offensive as some of these comments may have been, they are not, by a long shot, the most painful part of the trial process. During closing arguments, there was a moment where Charlie turned to the jury, and put forth the following question: "Mr. Zippel wants you to believe that he was sexually abused for a decade. Typically, abuse victims have all sorts of behavioral challenges, drug and alcohol issues, etc. He seems fine to me?" Thankfully, the jury in this case had enough common sense to realize that pain, scars, and disabilities are not only expressed by walking sticks, translators, and headphones. It is for that reason that we are thankfully, by the grace of God, where we are today. However, with Your Honor's permission, I would like a moment to address that comment, to answer that question:

To really understand the lifelong pain and torment suffered by survivors of childhood sexual abuse is to properly peek behind the curtain into the psyche of a survivor. There is a glaring misconception about sexual abuse that I feel desperately warrants correction. The reality of sexual abuse, as counterintuitive as its name may be, is not solely motivated by sex. At its core, sexual abuse is less about sex and more about power. The sexual high that a perpetrator enjoys while violating a child may last only a moment, but the power trip that they enjoy every moment of every day that they know that they have shunned an innocent soul into silence can last a lifetime. This provides powerful context into the entire dynamic of sexual abuse, and is a fact that easily answers a misinformed question at the heart of any sexual abuse trial. Why would a seemingly happily married, fifty-year-old mother of three want to engage in sexual activity with an eight-year-old boy? Was there something lacking in her relationship at home, that she somehow thought this child could supplement? I don't know the answer to that question, but what I do know is this: there is a serious lack of feeling of power in the life of every sexual predator, and it is that that they try to supplement by taking advantage of the most innocent and vulnerable in our society, by stealing power and control from those most unable to protect themselves.

How indeed does this dynamic play out? How does a sexual predator exert that kind of influence over a child, that can all at once scare them into silence and give the predator that feeling they crave? In my experience, it comes down to two things: fear and powerlessness. The more they can create those experiences in their victims, the more powerful they feel. But it's a process, and one that needs to be very carefully cultivated. It starts with what experts now call grooming. How do you take a child, born into a loving and caring family, a devout believer in a faith, and get him to remain silent regarding behavior that literally flies in the face of anything and everything he has ever stood for? You start with isolating him. You groom him into this behavior. You start creating cracks in his family dynamic, and find ways to slowly pull him away from his support structure. If you can see that he'll keep a small secret on your behalf, and not scurry off to tell his mommy about some gray area behavior you engaged in, then you can rest assured that he'll do the same after you pull him into the black. Each small episode, each tiny secret, each bond that brings the victim a little closer to his abuser and a little further away from his family, this is what sets the stage for sexual abuse to grow and flourish. As the abuse begins to get more and more bold, the victim experiences unbelievable amounts of fear. At trial, I testified about the fear of being discovered, what OTHER PEOPLE would do if they found out what I was up to. Truth be told, the fear that one has of others pales in comparison to the deepest and darkest fear of all. The fear of oneself. As a child, more than I was petrified of my parents, or friends, or teachers discovering my secret, I was paralyzed with the terror of myself. What kind of monster inhabited my mind, and lived in my body? What kind of gross, perverted, sexual deviant remained silent in the face of this behavior, not once or twice or ten times, but on a regular basis, and did nothing about it? Really, what was wrong with me? What world did I come from and what world did I belong in? I nauseated and disgusted myself to no end, and felt more alone and isolated than I can put into words. So I did what seemed like the only logical thing at that time. I ran back into the waiting and patient arms of my abuser. She was the only one in the entire world who could somehow legitimize what I was doing. She presented a purpose for what I was going through, a reason that she made an attempt to rationalize at every turn. She was the only one that really knew what was going on with me, and the adult-like feeling that she brought to me when she abused me was the only antidote to the intense pain that otherwise could not be numbed. It was at that point that she had found the second key that unlocked the next crucial dynamic of sexual abuse. Powerlessness. My abuser had set up a system where not only had she assured that her secret was safe with me, and that I would never in a million years betray her trust because of what that would mean for me, but more than that, I was now seeking out the abuse as much as she was. She had successfully and completely cut me off from every support system that was naturally given to me, and created a vacuum of safety and security that she was only too happy to fill. Sexual abuse is not so much about the momentary touching of a child's most private areas, or the purported romantic connection between abuser and abused. It's the feeling that the abuser gets after the encounter is over, and for every day and night that then passes, knowing that they have put a child into the ultimate winless situation. There is no chance that the child will tell, because the child is afraid of telling. In fact, the child is afraid of everything in their world at that point, themselves included. With one exception. The child is not afraid of the abuser. And so they come back. Time and again. Hating and detesting themselves in that moment for doing it, but only doing it because of how much they hate and detest themselves for having done it last time, and hoping that this time, this will be the last time, we promise ourselves, and this time will rid us, once and for all, of all the pain in our lives, just this one last time . . . until the next time, and the next time, and the next time.

And you know what, Your Honor, that pain doesn't fade. That self-loathing doesn't slow down. No, on the contrary, it grows and metastasizes and avalanches out of control with time. And as the years go on, that self-doubt, and inadequacy, and shaming and self-loathing . . . it rears its ugly head in every facet of our lives. Shame is the most pervasive negative emotion that we struggle with as human beings, and the toxicity that we have been buried under as children makes us carry that burden, every day, everywhere. In every relationship. In our personal lives. In our professional lives. In any and every choice we may have ever omitted or committed, that voice stays with us. That voice, born in a basement bathroom at a tender age, finds a permanent home within us, and uses the opportunity to speak up, welcomed or not, at any and every turn. You did this, it's your fault, you're a loser, you can't get your freaking ducks in a row, you're a pathetic excuse for a human being, always have been and always will be, to be honest. Your lack of character and conviction and inability to simply discern between right and wrong has been your Achilles heel for as long as you can remember and shows no sign of slowing down at all anytime soon.

Sometimes we're fortunate to talk down that voice. Some of us are lucky to re-engage with healthy support systems when we come forward, and are blessed with loving spouses, parents, siblings, and friends that give us the ability to quiet that voice down. But we're never able to shut it out. It never goes away. It sits and waits, most patiently, for a spark, for a kindred spirit, another voice that it can latch on to, and remind you of its constant presence. And then it finds it. In all places, in a court of law.

"Throughout this trial, the evidence will show that Mr. Zippel in fact initiated several of these encounters over the years," insinuates Joshua. "You WELCOMED these little encounters, didn't you? Over twenty-five percent of the time, that was YOUR testimony!" sneers Charlie. Yes, yes, I did, gentlemen. And trust me that not a day has gone by, or will ever go by, that I won't be reminded that at a tender age, I had the power to choose stripped from me by a sexual predator. From as far back as I can remember I had been put into a situation where I had the simple choice between what I was sure was right and very wrong taken from me by a person who had such a power deficiency in her own life that she needed to take that power from a young child to feel whole again. Yes, counselors, I was sexually abused and rendered powerless at eight. Thank you for so eloquently bringing that voice in my head back to life, and in the presence of my family and friends to boot. These, Your Honor, are the most painful moments of the trial process, liberally dousing salt into the wounds that we have been made to carry for a lifetime.

And yet, Your Honor, life moves on. And not just does it move on, with you or without you, but if you look closely enough, you have the good fortune, by the grace of God, to see precisely why each and every encounter happens in your life just the way it did. In fact, in light of all that has transpired in my life to this point, I consider myself the most fortunate human being alive on God's good earth, by virtue of the fact that I have had a front-row seat to see how I can be God's messenger in this world to bring about good from the abyss of negativity, to snatch joy from the jaws of despair. From very early on in this process, I was given the opportunity to realize that being a victim or a survivor of childhood sexual abuse is an intentional choice, which needs to be made regularly, and as I look around the courtroom today, how can I feel anything less than blessed to be a survivor? The staunch and unflinching support of my family, the remarkable heroes that I've had the chance to meet and form relationships with along the way, the superhuman public servants who have inspired me to passionately care for others in ways they'll never know, and the brave souls that I've had the merit to come in contact with, and be a stepping stone in their journey as survivors. I've learned first-hand and remind myself daily that my life is as good and wholesome as I'd like it to be that day; all it's really up to is how I want to see it.

It is with this in mind, Your Honor, that I ask the Court's permission to address my abuser at this point.

Vina, I must've been asked close to a thousand times if I was ready to see you in a jumpsuit and shackles this morning. Would that finally signify my victory and overcoming, reclaiming the upper hand after so many years? I never adequately answered that question to all those that had asked, but let me share with you what I was going to say to them.

The imbalance of power between us has been corrected for quite some time now. I say that as I remember that for close to eighteen years, from when you started abusing me up until recently, I could never look you in the eye. As a child, I remember getting a pit in my stomach each morning when you arrived for work, each time that you would show up at my house, after I'd returned from months at school, the same humiliating sensation, the same hot flush in my cheeks, and the same meek look down at my shoes, because I knew I couldn't meet your gaze. I always knew why, yet I could never put it into words. I knew then that if I would look into your eyes, I would see in myself what you saw in me. Your opinion and perception of me was the most valuable one I had in the world, you, you were teaching me to become a better husband one day, you alone who knew the deepest and darkest secrets of my soul. ... If I were to be reminded what you thought of me, there was no way I could ever think any different of myself.

May 9, 2018. Your initial appearance before this Court. Everybody, and I mean everybody, that was advising me had told me it was absolutely pointless to come to Court that morning. Your appearance before the judge would last all of ninety seconds; it was just a scheduling formality. But I had to be there. There was no way I was going to miss it. Because I was ready to meet your gaze once and for all. I finally felt enough about me, that my opinion of me, meant more than your opinion of me. I saw myself for who I was, and not for the version of myself you had created in both of our heads.

Where you had once looked at me and saw weakness, I looked at myself and saw strength.

Where you had once looked at me and saw terror, I looked at myself and saw courage.

Where you had once looked at me and saw shame, I looked at myself and saw hope.

Where you had once looked at me and saw powerlessness, I looked at myself and saw a reason to keep on fighting.

I came to court ready to look you in the eye and reclaim my image and self-worth. And on that day, and every day since then, for almost two years, you averted your gaze. Every single time. I don't need a jumpsuit and shackles to know that I've come out on top. The fact that I can look you right in the eye and you can't look back at me, that is a victory that can and will NEVER be taken from me.

Vina, you and I have been through a lot together over the years, but I want you to know this. Regardless of the duration of the sentence the Court hands down today, this is the very last time in my life that I ever hope to see you. And it is with that in mind that I want you to hear what I am about to say in the loudest, clearest, and most direct way possible, because I really and truly mean it with every fiber of my being.

Vina, I forgive you.

Now, I want to be clear. You have never asked for my forgiveness in any way, shape, or form. In fact, you have never remotely accepted any accountability for your actions, or owned anything you've done. Empowered by counsel, you lied and tried, shamed and blamed, told tales and sold stories, obfuscated and manipulated, and cast fault on anyone in the world aside for yourself. For the record, I have no doubt that even today, four months after a unanimous guilty verdict, you'll still try and pull one last one over on the judge.

But through it and notwithstanding it all, I forgive you.

I forgive you because I've learned that forgiveness is less about you and more about me.

I forgive you because I realize that in addition to the access to my body that you allowed yourself to for a decade, you've been living rent-free in my head for way longer than that. And I'm ready for that to stop today.

Vina, I'm certain beyond any reasonable doubt that at some point in your life you were deeply hurt by somebody, pain that far surpasses the normal parameters of suffering. And like so many in this world, and probably just like the person that hurt you, whether knowingly or unknowingly, you perpetuated that vicious cycle of violence. Like most hurt people, you went on to hurt people. And so on, and so on it continues. Until today. I refuse to let the cycle keep on spinning. The endless buck stops with me. Pain is a reality, but victimhood is a choice, and while I've been the recipient of the pain that you have passed on, I refuse to live another minute with the resentment, and anger, and frustration, and anxiety, and all of that, that comes with it. Today, I make the conscious choice to replace ALL of that negative energy with the dedication and commitment to more positively enhance the lives of others, specifically those whose life journeys look similar to mine. Instead of pain, I will find power to bring to others; instead of resentment, I will fight for myself and others with a renewed purpose; instead of being hurt, I make a choice to be healed.

I don't know, nor do I think I will ever, why God chose for this to happen to me, and why He chose for you to be the one to do it, but that's not something I'm going to worry about anymore. To be perfectly frank, Vina, I've got way too much good that I want to accomplish in this world than to waste my energy being angry at you, and so I forgive you. I am done thinking about the impact you have had on my life, and now I want to start thinking about the positive impact I can have on the lives of others. That is my impact statement.

Your Honor, if I may, I'd like to conclude with one last thought.

In Jewish Scripture we're taught that the best way to hope for another's forgiveness is to be merciful and forgive others when asked. With that in mind, I'd like to use this opportunity to ask for someone's forgiveness today. This is someone I'm not exactly able to address directly, so I've chosen to write them a letter, which I'd like to read now. The letter is dated September 1, 1999, and is addressed to an eight-year-old boy. This eight-year-old boy.

And it reads as follows:

Dear Avremi,

I am so, so sorry.

Let me be the bearer of bad news. Today, your life is going to change forever, and not in a good way. Today, a person entrusted with your care is going to wreak havoc on your pure and innocent eight-year-old soul, havoc from which you will never recover.

Why am I sorry? Because from this day forward, I've blamed you, my dear eight-year-old self. I've screamed at you, cried at you, cursed you for doing what you did, and blamed you for your choices. I'm sorry, because I've finally learned, IT WASN'T YOUR FAULT. YOU DID NOTHING WRONG. For some reason, God Almighty decided that this is the path that you will own through this life. You were a child and blindly trusted an adult, an adult who violated that trust and violated you forever. I'm sorry, little buddy. Today, the real culprit, the one who deserved all the screaming and shouting, the shaming and blaming that you've subjected yourself to over the past twenty years, today she finally pays the piper.

You're a great kid, and I'm sorry. I'm ready to let justice take it from here.

Acknowledgments

A list of everyone deserving of thanks and acknowledgment could not begin without giving wholehearted gratitude and appreciation to the Almighty God, He who gives strength to the weary and who dictates a path for each to walk on. "I'll follow Your plan; just don't let go of my hand."

I also feel it's important to acknowledge my Rebbe—the Lubavitcher Rebbe, Rabbi Menachem M. Schneerson, of saintly memory—who has given me the ability to see every space in the world as a vacancy waiting to be filled, and whose teachings have encouraged me to embrace a life-long journey of Shlichus in more ways than one.

To my dear wife, Sheina, who has taught me that "healing is a garden that is filled with thorns and weeds." This story is as much yours as it is mine, and you bring so much to it each day.

To my kiddos, who each contributed to this project in their own way—Immanuel, who occupied his permanent spot over my left shoulder, and read off words I didn't think possible for a seven-year-old; Menachem, who gave invaluable insight into the cover design process and who was happy to add his own hand-drawn versions when the options available weren't cutting it; and Sholom, who made his presence known to our family the same week that this book deal came together, and who's growth *in utero* rose alongside the words of this manuscript.

To my parents and siblings, who went down this road together with me and committed to heal together, grow together, and come together. None of this journey would have been possible without all of you in my corner.

To my in-laws and the entire Levin clan, who never expected any of this and certainly had no clue what they signed up for—thanks for joining along wholeheartedly.

To my Zaidy Schochet z"l, you should know that in your honor, I typed out all of Chapter 10 with my two index fingers, and I barely made it through. I don't know how you did it for an entire lifetime.

To Sergeant Kevin W. Blue of the Salt Lake City Police Department, you are a hero and everything right about the men and women in blue in every sense of the word. I wish every crime victim in the world to be fortunate enough to work with law enforcement like you.

To Senior Deputy District Attorney (and my new tour sidekick) Donna R. Kelly, who taught me what it means to care and what it means to fight. Guava Laffy Taffys forever.

To Amy Kershisnik, who carried the bag in more ways than one and always had whatever someone needed in more ways than one. Thanks for all the stair workouts.

To every public servant and rank and file member of the SLCPD, Salt Lake County District Attorney's Office, and the Matheson Courthouse who smiled, held a door, or just said "good morning" on tough days. You folks are what make the world go round.

To Elizabeth Smart, who taught me that real advocacy is putting your newborn in a car on a freezing day and schlepping to Starbucks to meet a perfect stranger. You've forged a path for all of us to walk down, and the life of anyone who shares a moment with you is richer for it.

To the trailblazers who lit a fire in me and in so many millions the world over with their selfless bravery and courage: Aly Raisman, Maggie Nichols, Jamie Dantzscher, Rachael Denhollander, and Sarah Klein. Keep shining your light!

To Gillian Friedman, who had the vision to see a story and the ability to develop the trust to make it happen.

To Tracey Tabet, who taught me that "call me whenever" means something else among friends, and Deondra Brown, who has shown me the power of a loud and effective voice. I'm glad I figured out what a Deondra is!

To Ann Marie Taliaferro, who reminded me that some defense attorneys do indeed have a heart and soul.

To Kara Robinson Chamberlain, who did what friends do: shared a good thing.

To Ryan Wekenman, the man who showed me that if you drill down to a soul level, two perfect strangers can find a common language they never knew.

To the entire amazing team at the Fedd Agency and Fedd Books:

The big boss, Esther Fedorkevich, who in one Zoom call displayed more confidence in my abilities than I ever had.

The agent extraordinaire, Tyler Spring, the greatest cheerleader and source of optimism ever known to mankind.

The jack of all trades and master of each of them, Mariah Swift, who made each step of this process meaningful, uplifting, and stress-free.

To Melissa Majchrzak, who did for this project what she does for any project—with patience and care she added an entirely new dimension of beauty, grace, and power.

To the members of the family at YJP and Chabad of Utah who read through the manuscript and gave insightful and rich feedback, your additions took this project to the next level. In particular, I'm grateful for Richard Kaplan, who played the role of my go-to counsel throughout this entire story, and Mort Fertel, who took on my book as his own.

Last, to my brother and sister survivors of every stripe and color the world over. This project is in honor of each and every single one of you. I hope you found some measure of solace in these pages and that it gave you some form of commitment to face your battles with the incredible strength and bravery that live on inside all of you. We didn't choose this life, but we can all be darn sure that it chose us for a reason. The light that we get to bring to this world is enormous. Keep shining on!